Español para los chiquitos

Spanish for Young Children
An Audio-Visual Course
for ages 4 to 7

Parent - Teacher Guide

Rita Wirkala, PhD

All Bilingual Press, LLC
Seattle, WA 98103
www.allbilingual.com

Printed by Morris Publishing
3212 East Highway 30, Kearney, NE 68847

LCCN: 2006910625
ISBN 13: 978-0-9745032-3-3
ISBN 10: 0-9745032-3-1

CONTENTS

INTRODUCTION

This method is designed to teach Spanish to children who do not yet read or are currently learning. The Parent/Teacher Guide explains how to use all the components of the method and lays out the lesson plans. The objective is to teach not only numbers, colors and animals, but to introduce a rich and relevant vocabulary in context, including common phrases for the target ages. It can be used either at home, with the help of the audio CDs, or in the classroom. This method is easily adaptable for multi-level classes where kindergartners and first graders learn alongside older children.

This *Parent/Teacher Guide* first suggests how to present new vocabulary based on the book's illustrations and CDs (see *The Children's Text* below). Next, the Guide offers a variety of activities such as games, drawing projects, TPR exercises, role playing, rhymes, songs, and other devices to reinforce the vocabulary and the simple grammar presented in the children's text. In explaining the activities, the Guide uses the classroom as a setting, but many of the activities can also be performed at home with some adaptation.

Importantly, to maintain the attention of the youngest students, the listening, speaking, writing, or drawing tasks alternate with physical activities.

Several activities require the use of "Bingo" and flash cards which can be prepared by the children themselves (see The Activity Book).

The Children's Text

The Children's Text is the Audio-visual text *Español para los chiquitos* which this *Parent/Teacher Guide* accompanies. It features illustrated words, sentences and expressions common to a child's daily vocabulary.
Activities based on the text match a corresponding illustration or figure with drawings, coloring, and vocalization in the form of dialogue or answers to questions in the audio-based lessons. Vocabulary words also appear in printed form next to the drawings for students who can read and to guide non Spanish-speaking parents. Some of the exercises encourage children to practice writing skills.

The Audio CDs

The audio CDs included with the children's text reproduce all the vocabulary and dialogues presented in the text. They also contain questions for teachers to ask students and the answers expected from the students, as well as rhymes and songs learned in class. In this way, the CDs simulate the role of a teacher for non Spanish-speaking parents.

The Activity Book

The *Activity Book* contains illustrations children can use to make flash cards of their own by cutting and coloring. It includes several blank grids and smaller illustrations for use in preparing bingo games.

Suggested Teaching Material Box

To facilitate class preparation we suggest that, at the beginning of the school year, teachers collect the following material for use throughout the year, and place these in a box to be kept in the classroom:

- Construction paper of different colors, and a few sheets of gold and silver paper.
- Drawing material such as crayons and colored pencils.
- Scissors and glue.
- A pair of dolls of different sizes and gender for use in naming clothing, body parts, and action.
- A pair of puppets to introduce new words and dialogue.
- Large poster paper for projects such as "the street", "the park", "the fields", etc.
- Double-sided tape, thumb tacks or magnets for children to place individual pictures on the board and walls.
- Beans or beads for bingo.
- Several balls.
- Old magazines on different subjects -- food, fashion, furniture, vehicles, architecture, nature.
- Old calendars for use in cutting out numbers.
- Candles, balloons, candy, plastic utensils, cups and plates for classroom parties.
- Pictures of your own family showing different generations.
- Modeling clay.

In a separate box, called "La caja mágica," you may want to have objects that represent vocabulary, such as:

- Toy animals, as many as you can collect, including spiders and snakes.
- Toy cars, trucks, motorcycles or other vehicles.
- Plastic fruits and other common foods.
- Play money for children's use in buying and selling objects.
- Doll clothes.

These items can be purchased cheaply at many toy or craft stores.

Unit 1: Mis primeras palabras

(My First Words)

Suggested toys: a cat, a teddy bear, a bear, 2 dogs (of different sizes) and a mouse.

Page 4

Presenting vocabulary

You can introduce the dialogue with two dolls or two puppets. One will be the mom or dad and the other will be the child. Before starting this or any other puppet presentation you will always say *"Miren,"* in this case, *Miren: la mamá, el papá, el nene, la nena,* etc.
Then you will use the command *"Escuchen."*
Show pictures of parents and children and ask students to repeat the vocabulary.

Dialogue

Distribute signs with the words *papá, mamá, nene, nena* and tape each one onto a child. Students who are *mamás* or *papás* look for *nenes* and *nenas,* and vice-versa, and practice the *"hola..."* greetings with each other.

1. ¿Qué animal es?

Using drawings or toys, teach the animal names used in this section. Use a cat, a teddy bear, a bear, a dog, and a mouse. Show the illustrations in the text, using the command *¡miren!*

Animal voices

- Say *¡escuchen!* and imitate each of the animal sounds. For example: *woof!woof! meaw, cuic cuic* [English *squeak, squeak*] and *grrrrr.* Ask students" *¿Qué animal es?* after each sound.

- Say the word in Spanish for any animal and ask the children to imitate its sound.

- Ask a child to choose an animal toy or picture, and then ask the class *¿Qué animal es?* The children should be able to identify each animal and answer in Spanish.

Writing

Copy the vocabulary words on the board and ask children to fill in the spaces provided on p.1 with the corresponding animal. Small children can start practicing writing by copying the letters.

2. Las vocales

Page 5

Pronunciation

Ask the children to look at the vowels printed on the page and the board, and repeat them after you. Exaggerate the position of the mouth (very closed, very open, etc.), always saying *"miren"* or *"escuchen."* If you are not a native or near-native speaker you can do this with the CD.
Point to each vowel in the book or the board and ask the children to pronounce it.

Writing
Ask the children to fill in the blanks with the missing vowels. For this, and any writing activity, you will use the command forms *"Vamos a escribir"* or *"Vamos a completar."*

Listening and drawing
For this, and future drawing activities, you will use the command form, *"Vamos a dibujar."* Pronounce (or play the CD) *osito, nene, nena, perro, gato, amigo, ratón, mamá.* After each word, ask the children to draw a picture in the cells. For example: *osito, #1.* When they all finish drawing, you can repeat the words, this time in different order, and ask children which cell number they are in.

3. Los números
Pages 6 and 7

Listening
Using the command *¡Escuchen!*, say the numbers from 1 to 10 (or play the CD). Ask the children to listen and repeat.
You will need to repeat the numbers many times until students learn them from 1 to 5, and from 6 to 10.

Writing
Using the command *Vamos a escribir,* have children draw the number inside the boxes next to the drawings in their text.

Speaking
Using the command *Vamos a hablar*, ask the children to say the numbers followed by the corresponding word. For example, *un ratón, dos gatos,* and so on.

Sitting in a circle
Have the children sit in a circle and count in Spanish (the first child will say *"uno"*, the second child will say *"dos"*, etc.). When you've gone around the circle once, try it again a little faster. You can have them try to count faster and faster each time.

4. ¿Cuántos hay? *(How many are there?)*
Page 8
Teach the question *¿Cuántos hay?* using objects in class.

¡Vengan! (Come!)
Assign a number to each child and call out: *1, 2 y 3, ¡Vengan!* Then ask the class, *¿Cuántos estudiantes hay?* Do the same with different numbers.

The diminutive
Teach each the diminutive. Say the words (or play the CD): *perro, perrito, gato, gatito,* etc. As you do so, ask the children to make "small" gestures if the word is in the diminutive and "big" gestures if it is not.

TPR (Total physical response)
Pronounce the words for each animal without the diminutive, while miming "big," and then say the corresponding diminutive miming "small." Then ask the children to tell you the diminutive form for each of the animals you call out while indicating with their hands big or small.

Speaking
Ask the children to look at the drawings in their texts and answer the question *¿Cuántos hay?* for each exercise on pages 8 and 9.

Working in pairs
Ask the children to perform a dialogue following the model:
-*¿Cuántos* perros *hay?*
-*Hay dos perros.*

The children will need to look at the relative size of the animals and be able to do say the word in diminutive.

Review activities

Page 9

Audio-visual activity
You or the CD will say a number and the children will draw a circle around each corresponding number in their text. For this and other listening and matching activities, use the commands *¡Atención! A escuchar y hacer un círculo.*

Listening and coloring
You or the CD will say the words and the children will color the six illustrations in their textbooks.

Game
For this and all other games, use the command *¡Vamos a jugar! (Let's play!).*
Give a piece of paper with a number written on it to each child.

Then say: *¡Atención! Número uno. ¡Ven!* (Come!); *Número cinco. ¡Ven!* etc.

A variation of this activity can be done outside, drawing ten circles on the pavement with a piece of chalk. When calling a number, the child has to run to the corresponding circle.

Counting voices

Divide the class into group A and group B. Whisper a different animal to each child from group A, which they will have to imitate. For example, two children will be dogs, and they have to say *guau guag,* four children will be cats, saying *miau miau,* three will be *ratoncitos,* saying *queek queek,* etc.

A speaker from Group A will say, *¿Cuántos perros hay aquí?*
Group B will answer, as a group: *Yo no sé, yo no sé.* (I don't know)
Group A will speak all the animal sounds out at once.
Group B will need to discern the different voices and figure out how many of each animal there are in group A. The answer should be given in complete sentences: *Hay dos perros,* or *hay tres gatos, etc.*

Repeat the game with other animals and be sure to have the groups change roles.

Bingo

In the activity book children will find blank grids, smaller illustrations, and numbers corresponding to this lesson. Each child will cut out one grid and several of the smaller illustrations/numbers and will glue them onto the blank grid. It is important that they glue the illustrations in a random order so that all of their grids have different combinations. Give the children some beans, or other place holders, and have one of them announce the numbers and animals The first child to get 3 or 4 beans in a row wins and gets to be the next announcer.

Unit 2: En la escuela

(At school)

Suggested materials: You will need a book, a notebook, a sheet of paper, a ruler, an eraser, a pencil, and several colored pencils. Also, beans for bingo.

1. En la clase *(In the classroom)*

Page 10

Presenting vocabulary

1. Use objects in the classroom to teach vocabulary by asking *¿Qué es?*
2. Ask the children to identify which drawing in their textbooks goes with which new word. Teach the word *conejo* (rabbit), and *conejito.*
3. Ask students to show the objects they have on their tables, using the words you have just given them.
4. Ask the children to take turns asking the class *¿Qué es?*

Pictionary

After the children become familiar with the new vocabulary, ask a child to draw one of the target words of his/her choice on the board or on paper while the others guess what it is in Spanish. English guesses don't count!

Cuántos* vs. *cuántas

Have the children look at the big illustration again, and ask them *¿Cuántos estudiantes hay? ¿Cuántos lápices hay? ¿Cuántos conejos hay?* Explain that objects ending in "a" such as "*goma*" or "*silla*" are feminine, so the question is "*CuántAs hay*" rather than *CuántOs hay.*

Page 11

Listening and drawing

Ask the children to draw the vocabulary words in the spaces provided in their texts. Say the words (or play the CD), show the object, and then repeat the word. After they are finished, look at individual drawings and ask *¿Qué es?* Older students can identify each object by writing its name underneath.

Hot potato

For this activity, say *Vamos a jugar a la "Papa Caliente"*

The children sit or stand in a circle and toss a teddy bear or other soft toy. Each time a child catches the toy, he/she has to say a Spanish word from the new vocabulary and then toss the toy to a classmate. That child must say a different Spanish word, toss the toy to another classmate, and so on.

2. Los colores *(The colors)*

Page 12

Presenting vocabulary

1. Teach the colors by showing the text illustrations of teddy bears.
2. With the aid of colored paper, pencils or crayons, and different objects in the classroom, to reinforce learning by asking *¿De qué color es?*
3. Test new vocabulary by asking students to show *un lápiz rojo, un lápiz verde,* etc.

Working in pairs

Ask the children to work in pairs and perform the dialogue by using the next four drawings in the text, following the model:

- *¿De qué color es?*
- *Es* ....

Ask the students to go back to page 9, show their drawings to their partners, and perform the same dialogue, this time adding the object names.

- *¿De qué color es el perro? ¿De qué color es el gato?* etc.

Listening and coloring

Ask children to color the numbers on p.12 with the color named by you (or the CD). For example: *"Pinten el número uno de rojo"*.

Page 13

Listening and coloring

Ask children to color the objects they hear with the color they hear. For example, you (or the CD) will say: *"Pinten el cuaderno de azul."*

3. ¿Cómo te llamas? *(What's your name?)*

Present the dialogue on p.13, if possible using a pair of puppets:
Then ask a volunteer to use the puppets to perform the dialogue.

Writing

Small children can start practicing the letters by writing their names in the space provided on p.13.

Speaking

Ask students to go around the classroom and perform the dialogue with others:

- *¿Cómo te llamas?*
- *Me llamo* ……………..

Ask them to change partners and practice the dialogue several times.

Sitting in a circle

Each student will ask the question to his/her neighbor until everybody has performed the dialogue.

¿Cómo se llama?

Ask the children to give names to toys (teddy bear named Teddy, dog named Bruno, etc.) Then ask, *¿Cómo se llama el osito?, ¿Cómo se llama el perro?, ¿Cómo se llama tu profesor/profesora?* Help children with the answers until they learn the pattern: *El osito se llama Teddy, El perro se llama Bruno,* etc.

Bingo with colors

Ask children to cut out a blank grid and color each cell with a different color. It is important that they choose randomly from the list of colors so that all of their grids have different color combinations.

Poem: *La vaca de mi amigo*

La vaca de mi amigo
Es blanca y marrón
No es vaca, es un toro
Y se llama Don Ramón
My friend's cow
is all white and brown
It's not a cow, it's a bull
and its name is Don Ramón

La gata de mi amigo
Es verde y violeta
Qué gata mas extraña...
¡Se llama La Coqueta!
My friend's cat
is all green and violet
What a strange cat!
Her name is The Coquette!

El oso de mi amigo
Es azul y anaranjado
Qué oso más chistoso
Se llama El Colorado
My friend's bear
Is blue and orange
What a funny bear,
His name is The Red One

El perro de mi amigo
Es blanco y amarillo
Es un perro muy peludo
Y se llama Don Cepillo
My friend's dog
is all white and yellow
It's a very hairy dog
And its name is Don Brush

El canario de mi amigo
Es negro, rojo y gris
Pues canta todo el día
Se llama DO RE MI
My friend's canary
is all black, red and grey
He sings the whole day
His name is DO RE MI

El pato de mi amigo
Es rojo, azul y negro.
Qué pato más bonito...
Se llama ¡No me acuerdo!
My friend's duck
Is all red, blue and black
What a pretty duck
His name is ...I forgot!

- Listen to the poem in the audio CD.

- Drawing: After listening to the poem once, go back to the beginning. Translate for the students and have them draw pictures to illustrate the animal words in the order they appear (first teach new words like *"vaca," "toro," "canario" and "pato").* Pause the CD player after each section so they will have a chance to complete the drawings. After all of them are finished, these drawings will help them memorize the lines of the poem and the sequence, by using the pictures as cues.

-For each step, use the commands *A escuchar, a dibujar* and *a recitar.*
(Parents can look up translations in the *Activity Book*)

Play Jeopardy, as it is explained in Appendix I.

Play "La gallina ciega" as it is explained in Appendix I.

Unit 3: En la tienda de ropas

(At the clothing store)

Suggested materials: Doll clothes (pants, shoes, jacket, shirt, T-shirt, tennis shoes, hat, dress, socks, and skirt); beans for bingo game; fashion magazines; scissors, glue and play money for every child.

Page 14

Presenting vocabulary

1. Ask students to repeat the vocabulary words by looking at the drawings.

2. Use clothing present in the class/home to reinforce vocabulary.

3. Ask the children to volunteer to ask the questions, using their own clothing.
¿Qué es? ¿De qué color es?

4. Use the illustration to review colors and numbers which will help them memorize the new vocabulary.
For example: *¿De qué color es la chaqueta? ¿De qué color son los calcetines? ¿Cuántos calcetines hay?*

5. Test vocabulary by asking *¿Qué hay en la tienda?* Encourage children to answer using *Hay un ...* or *una ...*

1. ¿Qué es esto?

Page 15

Dialogue

Encourage children to perform the dialogue using the items in the grid on p.15, and following the model above the grid.

Teaching the plural

Explain children that for items 6, 7, and 8 on the grid the answer should be "*son*" instead of "*es.*" It will be enough for now to tell them that "*son*" means *they are.*

Present the possessive "MI" using a pair of puppets if possible. One puppet will touch the other's clothing and ask *¿Qué es esto?* The other puppet will answer with the possessive "*mi*": *Es mi pantalón... Es mi chaqueta...*, etc.

Then ask a volunteer to use the puppets to perform the dialogue.

Listening and drawing

Students will use the next grid to draw the articles according to what they hear from you or the CD. They will use the illustrations above as a model.
After the activity is finished, you may look at each student's drawing and ask *¿Qué es esto?*

Review activities

¡Bingo! Play this game according to the instructions in the appendix.

Dressing the dummies

Give students big sheets of paper and ask each of them to draw an article of clothing. At the end you will need to have two sets of pants, shoes, shirts, hats, etc....
Put two-sided tape on the back of each picture. Divide the group into two teams, at random. Have two big dummies drawn on different parts of the board or on different boards. Have one announcer for each team say a word from the vocabulary. The child who has the picture corresponding to the article of clothing announced first has to run to the dummy and "dress" it -- that is, put it in the right place. The first team to dress the dummy completely is the winner.

Hot potato

For this activity say *Vamos a jugar a la "Papa Caliente"*
The children sit or stand in a circle and toss a teddy bear or other soft toy. Each time a child catches the toy, he/she has to say a Spanish word from the new vocabulary and toss the toy to a classmate. That child must say a different Spanish word, toss the toy to another classmate, and so on.

2. ¿Te gusta?

Page 16

Presenting vocabulary for *es pequeño, es grande, es feo, es bonito.*

- Use a big sheet of paper to teach "*Es grande*". Then cut off a corner of the paper, hold it up and say *"es pequeño"*. Use different objects in the classroom like pencils or stuffed animals to give more examples. Ask *¿Es grande o es pequeño?*

- Go back to Unit 1 and show the drawings for *perro, perrito, gato, gatito, ratón, ratoncito.*
Ask: *¿El perrito es grande o es pequeño? ¿El gato es grande o es pequeño?*

- Go to page 16 and show the pictures for "*grande*" and "*pequeño*". Ask: *¿Cómo es la camisa? ¿Es grande o pequeña?* Ask the same questions for both pictures and different items.

- Then teach *feo* and *bonito* with the next two pictures. Explain that *bonito* and *feo* are just opinions, and that there are no right or wrong answers.
Go to the Tienda illustration on p.14 and ask the children about each item of clothing. *¿Es bonito/a o es feo/a?*

- Introduce "*Me gusta*" and "*No me gusta*" using a pair of puppets if possible. One puppet will say *¿Te gusta mi chaqueta...?* (or any item the puppet is wearing) and the other will answer, *Si, me gusta, or No me gusta.*
Then ask a volunteer to use the puppets to perform the dialogue.

- Practice "*Me gusta*" and "*No me gusta*" together with "*es bonito*" and "*es feo*", using the pictures in the textbook. Then ask students the question *¿Te gusta?* for as many pictures as you have, starting with the ones that illustrate the four new words.

Writing
Students should practice writing the new vocabulary words while paying attention to the endings "o" versus "a." Remind them again about gender, pointing out that there is no gender for "e" endings such as *grande.*

3. ¿Cuánto es?
Page 17

Dialogue
Working in pairs: Have some magazines for the children to peruse, and choose different objects, such as an article of clothing, cars, foods or people, and play "tienda". One child will be the salesperson and the other the customer. Have play money to perform the transactions.

Salesperson: *¿Te gusta la camisa?*
Customer: *Sí. ¿Cuánto es?*
Salesperson: *10 pesos*
Customer: *Bueno, ¡toma!*

Ask students to trade objects.

Audio-visual activity
Call out the new adjectives (or play the CD): *pequeño, grande, bonito* and *feo,* and tell children to make a circle around the corresponding number next to the illustrations.

Spanish Tag
The child who is "it" says a Spanish word, such as "*zapatos*." Everyone runs away and when they duck down on the floor. In order not to be tagged they must say another word from the clothing lexicon, such as "*camisa*", etc. However, they can only stay down for 2 seconds. The child who is "it" has to run after another child, after which they get up and run again. Each child can only say a word once (they cannot say the same word every time).

Simón dice (*Simon says*)
Play "Simón dice" with the clothing items. For example:
Simón dice: toca la chaqueta, Simón dice: toca los zapatos; Simón dice: toca los pantalones, etc.

Rhythmic exercise.
Have children repeat following the rhythm, while pointing to each corresponding part of the body. For example, when they say *zapato* they should be touching their shoes; immediately they will go up and touch their pants while saying *pantalón*, and so on. The rhythm is slow at the beginning and then it should gradually increase until they can do it very fast.

Zapato, pantalón, camisa,
Pantalón, camisa,
Pantalón, camisa, gorro,
Camisa, gorro,
Gorro, camiseta, pantalón,
Camiseta, pantalón,
Camiseta, pantalón, zapatos,
Pantalón, zapatos.
Pantalón, zapatos, calcetines,
Zapatos, calcetines,
Calcetines, zapato, pantalón,
¡Y - ter - mi - no en - el - bo - tón!
(And I finish on the button)

Jeopardy
Play Jeopardy, first from Spanish to English and then from English to Spanish, as described on the Appendix to this Guide.

Al Gran Bonetón
Children can play *El Gran Bonetón* (as described in Appendix I) with any object from the vocabulary in this lesson. When playing this game for the first time, teach the verb "tiene".

La gallina ciega
Play *La gallina ciega* with any of the objects studied in this lesson and previous ones.

Unit 4: La familia

(The family)

Suggested materials: Candles, balloons of different colors, a bottle of juice, candies, a "*Feliz Cumpleaños*" sign, fake ice cream, and a gift-wrapped box. Pictures of teacher's family (2 or 3 generations if possible).

Page 18

Presenting vocabulary: La fiesta de cumpleaños *(The birthday party)*

-Have ready some *fiesta* items as suggested above. Ask the children to repeat the words, then point to the items one by one and ask: *¿Qué es esto?*

- Refresh the children's memory about question words:
¿Qué hay?, ¿Cuántos hay?, ¿De qué color es?

- Go back to the pictures and ask YES or NO questions (or use the CD). For example:
¿Qué hay en la mesa? Qué hay en la fiesta? ¿Hay un pastel en la fiesta? (pastel or *torta) ¿Hay helado en la mesa? ¿Hay globos en la fiesta? ¿Hay velas en el pastel? ¿Hay un perro en la clase? ¿Hay regalos en la mesa? ¿Cuántas personas hay? ¿Cuántos globos hay? ¿Cuántos regalos hay? ¿Cuántas velas (velitas) hay en el pastel? ¿De qué color es el globo número 1? ¿2? ¿ 3? ¿4? ¿5? ¿De qué color es el vestido de la abuela? ¿Hay un perro en la fiesta?*

To reinforce old vocabulary, ask similar questions about classroom items (have a few items on your table as per Unit 3).
¿Hay un pastel en mi mesa? ¿Hay globos en la clase? ¿Hay caramelos en mi mesa? Etc.

Page 19

Audio-visual activity
Say the vocabulary words in a different order than they appear on p. 19 (or play the CD) and ask children to circle the numbers according to what they hear.

Family members
Use the pictures to introduce vocabulary for family. Then, going back to the illustration on p.18, ask *¿Quién es? ¿El abuelo o el papa?¿La hermana o el hermano? ¿El abuelo o el nieto?¿el tío o la tía?* etc.

Writing
Reinforce the concept of gender by pointing out the ending vowels while children practice writing.

Hot potato
Sitting in a circle, play the game as suggested in the Appendix.
The children sit or stand in a circle and toss a teddy bear or other soft toy while saying one of the 10 words for family members: *papá, mamá, hermano, hermana, tío, tía, primo, prima, abuelo, abuela.*

Telling the age
Teach the expression *tiene* for age. Show again the picture on p.18 and say *"Laura tiene 6 años."* Ask each child his/her age. Ask children to fill in the blank with their age on p.19.

Dialogue
Encourage the students to perform the dialogue and answer in complete sentences: *"Tengo...."*

Page 20

At this point, the children already know *yo*. Now you can introduce *él* and *ella.* Bring pictures of your own family and show them to the class, saying their names.
For example: *Él es mi hermano. Se llama... Ella es mi ... Se llama....*

Drawing and writing
Ask children to draw different family members. Ask them to write *él* or *ella* according to gender. Ask each child: *¿Quién es él ? ¿Cómo se llama? ¿Quién es ella? ¿Cómo se llama?*

Children can bring family pictures for the next class, and perform the same exercises.

Writing
Ask children to copy the words for the pronouns *yo, él, ella.*

Review activities:

Page 21

Listening and running
Have a big sheet of paper on the board with an empty table drawn on it. Give each child a different object/flash card. Ask the children to run to the board when they hear the name of the object they have. For example, say: *¡Atencion! ¡el pastel! ven!* The child with the *pastel* has to run to the picture and place his/her object on it, with scotch tape or a thumbtack.

Audio visual activity.
Review of *"me gusta"* with cognates
First, have children pronounce the cognates, paying attention to the vowels: *"vainilla", "coco", "chocolate"," banana" and "limón".*
Using the pictures on p.21 of the textbook, have them write Sí or No under each of them, according to what they hear: You/the CD, will say: *¿Te gusta el pastel de banana? ¿Te gusta el helado de chocolate? ¿Te gusta el pastel de chocolate? ¿Te gusta el helado de vainilla?*

You may add other questions with known vocabulary: *¿Te gusta el helado de limón?¿... los caramelos? ¿Te gustan las fiestas de cumpleaños?*

Dialogues
Using the drawings on p.21, ask the children to work in pairs to perform the dialogue: *¿Te gusta...?* followed by the item shown in each cell.

Los amigos
Present the dialogue *"-Toma - Gracias"* with the pair of puppets, if possible. Then make the puppet give something to each child, so they will answer *"gracias,"* or *"no, gracias"*.

Dialogues
Encourage children to practice giving and thanking for something using *toma* and *gracias*. They may use any object in the class, or flash cards.

More vocabulary
Use two puppets to perform the action of kissing and hugging and saying *"Adiós"* Ask the children to repeat the new words. Ask for volunteers to perform the actions of hugging, kissing or saying *Adiós* with the puppets.

Writing
Ask children to copy the words on p.21.

Review vocabulary and introduce *"¿Quién dice?"* with the following questions:

¿Quién dice (says) *"gracias"?¿Luisito o la nena?*
What do you say in Spanish if you receive a present?
What do you say in Spanish when somebody leaves?

Song
Teach the Spanish version of *Happy Birthday* and sing the song each time there is a birthday in the class:

Cumpleaños feliz	*Happy birthday*
Te deseamos a ti	*We wish you*
¡Que los cumplas felices!	*Let be it a happy birthday!*
¡Cumpleaños feliz!	*Happy birthday!*

Red light-green light
Play this game as explained in Appendix I.

Unit 5: El cuerpo y las expresiones

(The body and the expressions)

Suggested materials: Large construction paper to make a dummy, and smaller sheets of paper for the children, double-sided tape and scissors for all.
Toys: a male and a female doll, and animals with four, two, many or no legs, such as a chicken or any bird, a snake or a worm, a dog, a cat, a spider, a rat, and a bear (you may wish to add other animals).

1. La cabeza

Page 22

Presenting vocabulary

Use the illustration in the text and your dolls, to teach vocabulary. Then ask children to imitate you while you touch parts of your head. Repeat the exercise several times.

"Simón dice"

Play this game using vocabulary for the different parts of the head. For example:
Simón dice: ¡Toquen la nariz! Simón dice: ¡Toquen las orejas!, etc.

Have a volunteer say the commands for "Simon dice…" for the whole class.

Writing

Point out the words ending in "s" to indicate plural nouns.

Working in pairs, ask children to point to the various parts of their heads and ask a classmate: *¿Qué es?*

Testing vocabulary

Have a volunteer go to the front of the class and ask, *¿Qué es?*, while touching his/her own face.

2. El cuerpo

Presenting more vocabulary

Use the illustrations in the text and your dolls to teach vocabulary. Then ask children to imitate you while you point to parts of your body. Repeat the exercise a few times.

"Simón dice"

Play the game in Spanish, saying the different parts of the body. For example:
Simón dice: ¡Toquen las piernas! Simón dice: ¡Toquen los brazos!, etc.

Writing
Point out that *mano* is a feminine word, and it is *la mano.*

3. ¿Cuántas patas tiene?
Page 23

Introduce "tengo" "tienes" "tiene"
Explain to the children that animals have *patas* by saying:

Los animales no tienen piernas, tiene <u>patas</u>. Y tienen <u>cola</u> (tail)

¿Cuántas patas?
- Use the toys, and say *él* or *ella tiene.... patas.*
- Ask the students to look at the animal drawings in the text on p.52 and say:
¿Cuántas patas tiene el pájaro?
¿Cuántas patas tiene el ratón? ¿Él tiene cola?
¿Cuántas patas tiene la serpiente? ¿Ella tiene cola?

Use pronouns *él* and *ella* for the animals, to reinforce previous lessons.

- Teach the children the position of the negative. For example:
La araña <u>no tiene cola</u>.

- Teach the children the adverbs *mucho, mucha, muchos, muchas.*
For example: *La araña tiene muchas patas.*
Repeat the questions for as many animals as you have.

Dialogue
Working in pairs, ask the children to perform the dialogues according to the pictures on p.23 of the text. Give the children the model for the dialogue and have them answer in short sentences:
- *¿Cuántas patas tiene el perro?*
- *Tiene cuatro.*
-*¿ Él tiene cola?*
- *Sí, tiene cola.*

Encourage them to proceed with the other animals: *gato, oso, pájaro, ratón y serpiente,* always paying attention to the negative form: *"no tiene".*

Repeat the exercise with *"dientes"*. Ask students:
¿Qué animales tienen dientes? Use the toys or the drawings and answer with *Sí, tiene* or *No, no tiene.*

For example: *¿El perro tiene dientes?*
Use cognates that are easily recognized by children. For example:
¿El canario tiene dientes? ¿El mosquito tiene dientes?

El extraterrestre
Divide the class into two teams. Using recycled paper if possible, ask students to draw eyes, ears, mouths, and noses, (all parts of the head) at random, and then cut the figures and put double-sided tape on the back. Have two dummies with big heads (low enough for small children to reach) or draw them on the board, <u>but without features</u>. Have 2 children announce the words for each of their teams. Children who have the announced parts will run and place them on the dummy's head. Since there might be more than two eyes or ears or more than one mouth, the final result will be the "extraterrestre".
Ask children to decide who is *"el más feo"* or *"el más bonito"*.
Ask them to invent a name for each one.
Then, ask the class:
¿Cuántos ojos tiene el extraterrestre #1? ¿Cuántas orejas tiene? ¿Cuántas bocas tiene? ¿Cuántas narices tiene? ¿Cómo se llama él?
Repeat the questions for figure #2.

Pin the tail on the extraterrestre
- Draw 4 or 5 legs, 4 or 5 arms, 4 or 5 hands, and 2 heads on construction or poster paper. Double the amounts if the class is large and divide it into two teams. Give the papers to the class to cut out, always using the target language: *corta la pierna, corta la mano, corta la cabeza,* etc.
Have another dummy (or two) ready, this time without arms/legs or head. Give each child a part to cut out. Then say *¿Quién tiene una pierna? ¿Quién tiene una mano?¿Quien tiene una cabeza?* etc.

- Ask a volunteer to pin the part on the dummy. Before blindfolding the child, encourage him/her to talk, asking things like *¿Qué tienes?¿Una mano?* Allow enough time for the child to think about where to place the cutout. After all of the students have had a chance to put their part on the dummy, the result will probably look like another extraterrestrial figure. Ask students *¿Cómo se llama?*

Review activities:

<u>Being creative</u>
- Ask children to draw their own extraterrestrial creature or robot in the space provided in the text, and invite them to the front of the class to say, with your help, something like *mi robot tiene cuatro brazos, tres piernas,* etc.

- Have students ask the presenter for the name of his/her "extraterrestre" or robot.
Children may save their drawings for the next day to review the parts of the body.

TPR and Song
Teach the word *hombros.* Then model the physical movements while saying the words, actually touching your head, face, legs, feet, etc. Do it rhythmically.

Repeat each sentence 2 or 3 times.

Cabeza, cuello, brazos... cuello, brazos.	(Repeat)
Rodillas, piernas, pies...piernas pies	(Repeat)
Ojos, boca, dientes... boca, dientes	(Repeat)
Cabeza, orejas, nariz... orejas, nariz.	(Repeat)
Cara, brazos, manos... brazos mano.	(Repeat)

To finish:
¡Cabeza, cara, hombros, pies!

Have the children do the exercises several times, first slowly and then faster and faster.
Once the children have learned the exercises, play the CD for them to add music to the rhythm.
They will learn the melody fast and will be able to sing along with the CD.

Hot potato
Sitting in a circle, play the game as suggested in Appendix I.

¿Cómo se dice?
Have a child go to the front and, while pointing to parts of the body, ask the class:
¿Qué es? ¿Cómo se dice?

4. ¿Cómo estás?
Page 24

Presenting vocabulary
Use the puppets to introduce *Estás* and *Estoy.* One puppet would ask the other *¿cómo estás?* The second would answer with the variations *bien, más o menos, mal....* Try to use the expression of your voice to convey the different feelings.
Show the pictures on p. 24 of the text and teach the words:
está bien – está cansado - está regular or *más o menos –está mal.*

Draw four faces on the board and repeat the words. Then ask the class *¿Cómo está?* for each of your drawings.

Ask each child, "*¿Cómo estás?*" and point to the faces on the board, repeating the words to help them with their answers.

Encourage a volunteer to perform the dialogue with the puppets.

¿Cómo está la muñeca?

Looking at the pictures of the three dolls on p.24, ask the class:
¿De qué color es el pelo de la muñeca? ¿Tiene pantalón o vestido? ¿De qué color es?

- Review vocabulary by asking *¿cómo está la muñeca?* for # 1 and #2, and then add the new one: *triste, contenta* and *enojada.*
- Ask several volunteers to draw a face on the board and ask the class *¿Cómo está?* Make sure that all the learned expressions are represented.
- Then go back to the three pictures and add the expressions *¡Pobrecita! ¡Qué bueno!* and *¡Qué pena…!*

Tell the class to look at picture #1, and say:
La muñeca está triste. ¿Qué decimos? (What do we say?)
- *¡Pobrecita!*
Repeat the exercise with the other expressions.

Review activities

Page 25

Audio-Visual activity

Have the children circle the numbers corresponding to the faces, according to what they hear from you or the CD:

Está contenta. ¡Qué bueno!
Está triste. ¡Qué pena! or *Pobrecito!*
Está enojada. ¡Qué pena!
Está cansado. ¡Pobrecito!

Drawing

Teach the adverb "MUY" (*very*) which they can use before any of the learned adjectives. Have children draw their own faces in the spaces provided on p. 25 for the expressions written in each cell, which you will read for them.

Dialogue *¿Cómo estoy?*

Working in pairs, a child will make a face expressing happiness, anger, sadness, great joy, tiredness, etc., and ask the other *¿Cómo estoy?*
Alternatively, they may design masks with simple faces showing the various expressions, and ask the same question.

Play **Bingo** with all the nouns learned so far.

Unit 6: En la casa

(At home)

Suggested materials: Magazines from home, soap, towel.
Toys: sofa, bed, stove, chair, table, flowers, bathtub. Modeling clay.

1. Los cuartos y los muebles

Page 26

Presenting vocabulary

- If possible, use a doll house to teach new vocabulary. Use also the text picture to teach the rooms: *la cocina, la sala, el baño, el dormitorio.*

- Ask: *¿Qué hay en la casa* (or *en la casa de la muñeca?) ¿Hay una cocina? ¿Hay un garage?* etc. *¿Es bonita? ¿Te gusta?*

Page 27

Writing and Drawing

First let children practice their writing by copying the words on p. 27. Then say the same words, one at a time, and ask children to draw the rooms in the house below. Simple line sketches delineating each room will be enough.

2. ¿Dónde está? ¿Dónde estás? ¿Dónde estoy?

Page 28 and 29

- Teach *dónde* and *aquí* vs. *allá*
Go around the class and, using the previous drawing activity, ask:
¿Dónde está la cocina? ¿Dónde está la sala?, etc., prompting the answer *¡Aquí!*

- Pantomime someone sleeping, cooking, washing or reading a book. For each mimicked action, ask: *¿Dónde estoy? ¿En el dormitorio o en el baño? ¿En la sala o en la cocina?*

- Ask for volunteers to come to the front and mime actions while asking the class: *¿Dónde estoy?*

- Encourage children to do the same exercise in pairs.

- Use the exercises to reinforce personal pronouns. Join the students and perform the action yourself, asking, *¿Dónde estoy yo? ¿Dónde está él? ¿Dónde está ella?*

Más palabras

-Use features of the classroom to teach *puerta, ventana,* and real or pictured flowers to teach *flores.* Go to the picture and show the words again, including *escalera.*

-Look around the classroom and ask:

¿Hay una puerta? ¿Hay una ventana? ¿Cuántas puertas hay aquí? ¿Cuántas ventanas hay aquí? ¿Hay un jardín en la escuela? ¿Hay flores en el jardín? ¿Hay un baño? ¿una cocina? ¿una escalera? Etc.

On the board, draw windows and doors of different sizes. Ask:

Esta puerta, ¿Es pequeña o es grande? Esta ventana, ¿Es pequeña o es grande?

Drawing

Ask children to draw a rectangle on a big piece of paper, as if it were the exterior shape of a school. Ask them to draw doors and windows of different sizes with gardens in front. For example: *una puerta grande, una puerta pequeña, cuatro ventanas pequeñas y dos ventanas grandes, un jardín con flores.* Then go around the class and ask, *¿Esta puerta es pequeña o es grande? ¿Este jardín tiene flores? ¿Es bonito?* Etc.

Furniture

- Use the big picture on p. 26 to teach furniture, one room at a time. Use your toys, if you have them, or model some with clay, and ask *¿Qué es?*

- On p. 28, do a dialogue using the pictures.

For example: *- ¿Dónde está el sillón? - Está en la sala.*

- Use the text illustration on p. 29 for the bathroom vocabulary.
  Ask *¿Dónde está el nene?*

Furnishing the house

- Give each child four sheets of paper, one for each room: *la cocina, la sala, el baño, el dormitorio.* Put the four words on the board and ask the children to copy one word on the top of each page.
- Provide old magazines for children to cut out different pieces of furniture, or ask them to cut out the corresponding flash cards from their Activity Book. Children can work on this project for a few days, adding furniture for each room, item by item. For example, say, "we are going to put *una mesa y unas sillas en la cocina; busquen mesa y sillas.*
- Ask children to repeat the word each time they find a picture before gluing it onto the page.
- Repeat this activity for *la sala, el baño* and *el dormitorio.* Go around the class looking at the pages and ask *¿Qué es?* Have older children write the name of the furniture underneath. Smaller children can copy the words from the board.

Audio-visual activity

On p.29, have children circle the number that corresponds to the picture according to what they hear.

For example, say: *jardín, estufa, flores , sillón , escalera, puerta, cama, jabón, ventana, bañera, toalla.*

Then ask: *¿Qué número es el ....la.....?*

Review activities

¿Dónde está?

Ask children to look at the picture on p.28 and ask:
¿Dónde está la cama? ¿Dónde está la televisión? ¿Dónde está el sillón? ¿Dónde está la bañera? ¿Dónde están las flores?

Play *Hot potato, Bingo, Gallina Ciega* or *Red Light Green light.*

Song:

El hornero is an Argentinean bird that makes his home with mud and straw. His house is very elaborate, because it has several rooms. Children can color the *hornero's* house on p.28 and then learn the poem. After having learned the poem they can learn the song, listening to the CD.

La casita del hornero

La casita del hornero	*The "hornero's" little house*
Tiene sala y comedor	*has living room and dining room*
Tiene baño y cocina	*It has bathroom and a kitchen,*
Dormitorio y un corredor	*bedroom and corridor.*
Por la noche entra la luna	*At night enters the moon*
Por la tarde entra el sol	*In the afternoon enters the sun.*
La casita del hornero	*The "hornero's" little house*
Tiene silla y sillón	*has chair and armchair*
Tiene techo y tiene piso	*It has roof and it has floor*
Y es redonda y marrón.	*and it is round and brown.*
Por la noche entra la luna	*At night enters the moon*
Por la tarde entra el sol	*In the afternoon enters the sun.*
La casita del hornero	*The "hornero's" little house*
Tiene puerta y portón	*has door and it has gate,*
Tiene hierbas perfumadas	*It has fragrant herbs*
Y una flor en el balcón.	*And a flower in the balcony;*
Por la noche entra la luna	*At night enters the moon*
Por la tarde entra el sol	*At evening enters the sun.*

El Gran Bonetón

Children can play the *Gran Bonetón* as described in the Appendix with selected flash cards from their Activity Book.

Jeopardy

Play Jeopardy first from Spanish to English and then from English to Spanish as described at the end of this Manual.

Building a house

Have a big box for every 4 or 5 students, and a cat on one side. Each box will be a room. Then if you have enough toys, ask each team to look for the "furniture" that corresponds to their room -- or, students can make their furniture from modeling clay. Be sure that they use the target language when they place the furniture, saying:
Aquí está la cama. Aquí está el sillón, etc.

Unit 7: ¡A comer!

(Let's eat!)

<u>Suggested Materials</u>: Real food (fruit, salt, sugar, boiled eggs, bread); an empty milk carton, paper or plastic plates, forks, spoons, cups, mugs and knives. Plastic fruit or any other food. Newspapers with ads for food. Beans.

1. En la mesa

Page 30

Presenting vocabulary

- Use your props to teach vocabulary, first the utensils and then the food.
Reinforce utensil vocabulary asking *¿Qué es? ¿Es un tenedor o un cuchillo? ¿Es un vaso o una taza?*

- Ask children to identify utensils in the picture, asking:
¿Hay platos en la mesa? ¿Cuántos hay? ¿Hay tenedores en la mesa ¿Hay vasos en la mesa? ¿Cuántos hay? etc.

- Have a child go to the front to take paper utensils and plates or plastic utensils from the table and ask the class: *¿Qué es?*

- Teach food words in groups of three or four. Then test vocabulary
using the pictures. For this exercise, teach the negative *No hay*, and ask questions related to any food items, even if not in the picture, to prompt the answers in positive and negative form.
For example:
¿Hay manzanas en la mesa? ¿Hay uvas en la mesa?
Repeat the exercise with other food groups.

- After children have managed several words for each group, try these questions.
For the first food group:
What do we need to eat a *sopa?* To cut *una naranja?* To eat a *papa?*
¿El cuchillo, la cuchara o el tenedor?

For the second food group:
What do we need to drink *café con leche*? *¿Un vaso o una taza?* Y...¿agua? Y...*¿jugo de naranja?*

For the third food group:
What do we put *en la leche? ¿Azúcar o sal? Y en la sopa ¿ Azúcar o sal?*

Drawing
Ask children to draw utensils on the table according to what they hear. For example, you can start by telling the kids to draw the plates and silverware, then mention other utensils and, finally, the food.
Go around the class and ask each student *¿Qué es?*

Pictionary
Ask children to do their own drawings and ask a partner (or the group): *¿Qué es?*

Tasting
Have an apple, an orange and a banana. Cut them in little pieces and put them on a plate. Ask a volunteer to "try" the fruit. With blindfolded eyes, the child has to pick a piece of fruit and say the name in Spanish.

2. ¿Qué te gusta comer? ¿Qué quieres comer?

Review *"Me gusta"* and *"Te gusta"*. Introduce *"Le gusta"*.
Go back to the picture and while showing the first child, saying:
Le gusta, quiere más. Dice "¡Qué rico!"
For the second child, say *le gusta mucho. ¡Está delicioso!*
For the third child says *¡No le gusta!*

Page 31

-Ask children: *¿Te gusta la manzana? ¿La banana? ¿La naranja? ¿La leche? ¿La sopa? ¿Qué te gusta comer?*

- Have children perform the dialogue with different foods, following the model.
- *¿Te gusta el helado?*
- *Sí, me gusta.*
    - *¿Te gusta el hígado* (liver)*?*
    -*No, no me gusta. ¡Es horrible!*

- Do the same dialogue, introducing *¿Quieres? No quiero…*

Audio-visual activity
Say the vocabulary words one at a time (or play the CD) and ask them to circle the corresponding number according to what they hear. After each word ask, *¿Qué número es el / la…?*

Guessing
Ask students to guess the name according to color and shape, etc.

For example:
Es una fruta, es anaranjada.¿Qué es?
Es para tomar agua (mimic the action of drinking). *¿Qué es?*
Es para cortar (mimic the action of cutting). *¿Qué es?*
Es para tomar la sopa (mimic the movement and noise of eating soup). *¿Qué es?*
Es una fruta, roja o verde (show the picture above). *¿Qué es?*

Hot potato
Sitting in a circle, play the game as suggested in Appendix I.

3. Tengo hambre. Tengo sed.
Page 32

Presenting vocabulary and expressions
- Pointing at each illustration, say:
El gatito tiene hambre. He says: *¡Tengo hambre!*
El pájaro tiene sed. He says: *¡Tengo sed!*
El osito quiere helado. Dice: ¡Está frío!
El gato quiere sopa. Dice: ¡Está caliente!

- Repeat the vocabulary with your puppets. One will touch his/her tummy saying *tengo hambre* and the other will offer something saying *come un …*or *una …;* or *tengo sed,* and the other will say *¡toma agua!*

-Go back to the figures in the text and say: *El gatito tiene hambre. ¿Qué dice?* and repeat the questions for each of the four animals.

-Ask the following questions, helping with the answers:

If you want *agua,* what do you say? *Tengo …*
If you want *pizza,* what do you say? *Tengo …*
If the *sopa* is hot, what do you say? *Está …*
If the *sopa* is cold, what do you say? *Está …*

- Ask *Sí / No* questions, using *quieres* and *te gusta.* For example:
¿Quieres sopa fría? ¿Te gusta la sopa fría? ¿Quieres helado caliente?¿Te gusta el helado caliente?
¿Quieres pizza caliente? ¿Te gusta la pizza caliente?

Audio-visual activity
Ask children to look at the pictures and circle the number that corresponds to what they hear from you or the CD. Check the answers afterwards.

1. *Tengo hambre. Quiero <u>comer</u> un sándwich.*
2. *La sopa está caliente.*
3. *Tengo sed. Quiero agua fría.*
4. *Tengo sed. Quiero un jugo.*

Page 33

- Ask children to copy the sentences *Me gusta* or *Me gusta mucho,* or *¡Qué rico!* Or *No me gusta,* for each food item below. Repeat the words until non-readers can identify them.

Dialogue
Ask children to perform the dialog on p. 33 and help them write their answers.

Review exercises

TPR. *Simón dice*:
Play *Simón dice* with the new vocabulary. Ask children to mimic the actions. For example: *Toma agua, come un sándwich, toma la sopa, corta una naranja…*

Bingo
Ask each child to cut a bingo sheet from their Activity Book and cut and glue the vocabulary words for food, one in each box, at random. Children can add more food by cutting pictures from magazines. Go around the class and ask of each one, *¿Qué es?* before starting the game.

Setting the table
Ask children to cut the vocabulary flash cards from the Activity Book, and other food from magazines. Have a big sheet of poster paper on the board, with an empty table drawn on it, or draw your table directly on the board. Say the word and call the child. For example: *¡Atencion! ¡la manzana, ven!* The child with the *manzana* has to run to the picture and place the corresponding flash card on the table.

Play Spanish tag with vocabulary

More dialog
- Put all the food and other flash cards that the children have cut out on the table. They can perform the dialogue:
Student 1 *¿Te gusta……(name of the food/flash card)?*
Student 2 *Sí, me gusta,* or *No me gusta.*
If student 2 says *Si, me gusta,* student 1 hands over the card, saying *¡Toma!*

- Review the verb *"quieres"*, offering children play food, saying: *¿Quieres un chocolate? ¿Quieres un caramelo?¿Quieres una banana? etc.*
Encourage children to continue the charade saying

Mmm, ¡qué rico! *¡Me gusta!* Or *No me gusta…*
- Have the children perform the dialogues using puppets.
- Play *restaurante* in groups, performing variations of this dialogue:

-Tengo hambre *-¿Qué quieres comer?* *- ¡Carne!*

Rhyme : Con el cuchillo

YO
Con el cuchillo
Yo corto la fruta
Con el cuchillo
¡Sí señor!
With the knife
I cut the fruit
With the knife,
Yes, Sir!
TÚ
Con el cuchillo
Tú cortas la fruta
Con el cuchillo
¡Sí señor!
MI AMIGO
Con el cuchillo
Él corta la fruta
Con el cuchillo
¡Sí señor!
NOSOTROS
Con el cuchillo
Cortamos la fruta
Con el cuchillo
¡Sí señor!

MIS AMIGOS
Con el cuchillo
ellos cortan la fruta
Con el cuchillo
¡Sí señor!

YO
Con la cuchara
Yo tomo la sopa
Con la cuchara
¡Sí señor!
With the spoon
I sip the soup,
With the spoon
Yes, Sir!
TÚ
Con la cuchara
Tú tomas la sopa
Con la cuchara
¡Sí señor!
MI AMIGO
Con la cuchara
Él toma la sopa
Con la cuchara
¡Sí señor!
NOSOTROS
Con la cuchara
Tomamos la sopa
Con la cuchara
¡Sí señor!

MIS AMIGOS
Con la cuchara
ellos toman la sopa
Con la cuchara
¡Sí señor!

YO
Con el helado
Yo uso la lengua
Con el helado
¡No uso el tenedor!
With the ice cream
I use the tongue,
With the ice cream,
Yes, Sir!
TÚ
Con el helado
Tú usas la lengua
Con el helado
¡No usas tenedor!
MI AMIGO
Con el helado
Él usa la lengua
Con el helado
¡No usa tenedor!
NOSOTROS
Con el helado
Usamos la lengua
Con el helado
¡No usamos tenedor!
MIS AMIGOS
Con el helado
ellos usan la lengua
Con el helado
¡No usan tenedor!
¡NO SEÑOR!

Before this activity, explain some rudimentary grammar.
Review the verbs *tomar, cortar,* introduce *usar,* and explain the use of the endings

"o" for *yo,* "s" for *tú,* "a" for *él* or *ella.*

Ask students to mimic using a knife, a spoon or licking an ice cream cone.
Then ask them to draw a fruit, a bowl of soup and an ice cream cone to go with the following verses.

Unit 8: En el parque

(In the park)

Suggested Material: Two puppets
Toys: ball, pacifier, bike, roller skates.

1. La gente en el parque

Page 34

Presenting vocabulary

Using the illustration, teach *parque, lago, señor, señora, chico, chica, bebé, bicicleta, triciclo, sol* and *árbol.*
Give examples with names of parks or lakes in your area. Ask children:
¿Do you know any *lago?* ¿Do you know any *parque?*
Ask questions about the picture: *¿Qué hay en el lago? ¿Hay flores? ¿Cuántas personas hay? ¿De qué color es la ropa del chico? ¿Dónde está el nene ? ¿Te gusta el parque?*

Writing

Ask children to copy the words in the space provided. Call their attention to the endings *-os and –as* for plural masculine and feminine (*chicos* and *chicas*).

Page 35

Audio-visual activity

Go over the vocabulary words (or play the CD) one at a time and ask the children to circle the corresponding number according to what they hear. After each word ask, *¿Qué número es el...la...?* This excercise is only to identify nouns, not actions.

2. Llueve... Hace sol.

Page 36

More sentences

- Indicate the sun and say: *Hay sol* or *Hace sol. ¡Es un buen día!*
- Draw a sun on the board and repeat: *¡Es un buen día! ¡Es un día bonito!*
- Do the same with "llueve" and "arco iris".
- Then add the sentences and ask them to guess what we say for each situation.
For example: *Llueve en el parque. ¿Qué decimos?*

Drawing
-Tell children to draw the sun, the rain and the rainbow in the spaces provided. Then go around the class and ask with regard to each drawing, *¿Dónde está el sol? ¿El arco iris? ¿La lluvia? ¿Es un buen día? ¿Llueve o hace sol?*
- Ask them *¿Qué decimos cuando llueve? ¿Y cuando sale el sol? ¿Y cuando sale el arco iris?*

3.¿Qué hacen?

Presenting actions
- Teach the verbs that appear in the illustration on p.34, mimicking the actions with body motions when possible, or use of puppets. Then ask the children to look at the picture. Show the actions, saying:

Esta chica anda en bicicleta. Este chico juega a la pelota. Este señor camina y habla con el chico. La chica lee. El chico y la chica corren. La chica patina. La señora saluda a la amiga. El nene anda en triciclo. Él tiene el chupete. La nena pasea con el perro. El bebé llora. ¡Quiere el chupete! El bebé dice "¡Dame mi chupete!

- Ask children to repeat the verbs and imitate you or the puppets. Verbs like *jugar a la pelota, leer, correr, saludar, pasear con el perro* and *llorar* are easily performed .

- Go back to the picture and ask the children, *¿Qué hace el chico? ¿Anda en bicicleta o juega a la pelota? ¿Qué hace el señor? ¿Corre o camina? ¿Qué hace el bebé? ¿Habla o llora? ¿Qué hace la señora? ¿Quién anda en bicicleta? ¿Quién anda en triciclo?*, etc.

TPR
Play *Simón dice* with the actions. Give the new verbs in two stages, three or four at a time, until the children can recall them. For example:

Simón dice: "corre"; Simón dice: "camina"; Simón dice: "anda en bicicleta"; Simón dice: "anda en triciclo".
Then proceed to the other group
Simón dice: "habla"; Simón dice: "llora"; Simón dice: "pasea con el perro"; etc.

Page 37

Audio-visual Activity
Ask children to circle the number corresponding to the action they hear. For example:
Llora, anda en bicicleta, lee, camina y habla, juega a la pelota, corre, patina, saluda, pasea con el perro.
Then check the answers.

Review activities

Drawing

Have children draw their own park. Tell them what to do using the vocabulary: *Dibujen un lago. Dibujen 3 patitos en el lago. Dibujen 3 chicos, un señor, una señora,* etc.
Go around the class and ask each child about a particular part of the drawing:
¿Qué es? ¿Quién es?

Making a park

Hang a large sheet of poster paper on the board. Ask children to prepare one or two flash cards at random by cutting them out of their Activity Book. Make sure that all the actions are represented.
When you say the words for a certain action, the child or children with the picture will come to the board and place it on the "park" with scotch tape or other device.

Charade

- Working in pairs, one child mimics an action while the other tries to guess what the action is. For example, *"corre"*, *"camina"*, *"patina"*, *"llora"*, etc.

- Have one volunteer go to the front and mimic an action, then ask the class *¿Qué hace...?* (Say the child's name.)
- Play any of the games already known as explained in Appendix I.

Song

Learn our version of *La Cucaracha.* Before teaching the lyrics, go over the known verbs. Present vocabulary:

puede = he/she can
no puede = he/she cannot
le falta = he /she is lacking
de atrás = behind, rear (legs)
perezoso/a = lazy

Then listen to the song (next page) on the CD and use it to review personal pronouns and verbs.

La cucaracha

I

La cucaracha, la cucaracha,
ya no puede CAMINAR
porque no tiene, porque le faltan
las dos patitas de atrás
Cucaracha, cucaracha,
no seas tan perezosa,
mira como yo camino,
y no tengo más que dos.[1]

II

La cucaracha, la cucaracha
ya no puede PATINAR
porque no tiene, porque le faltan
las dos patitas de atrás.
Cucaracha, cucaracha,
no seas tan perezosa,
mira como yo PATINO
y no tengo más que dos.

III

La cucaracha, la cucaracha,
ya no puede MÁS PASEAR,
porque no tiene, porque le faltan
las dos patitas de atrás.
Cucaracha, cucaracha,
no seas tan perezosa,
mira como yo PASEO
y no tengo más que dos.

IV

La cucaracha, la cucaracha,
ya no puede CORRER,
porque no tiene, porque le faltan
las dos patitas de atrás.
Cucaracha, cucaracha,
no seas tan perezosa,
mira como ELLOS CORREN
y no TIENEN más que dos.

V

La cucaracha, la cucaracha,
ya no puede MÁS JUGAR,
porque no tiene, porque le faltan,
las dos patitas de atrás.
Cucaracha, cucaracha,
no seas tan perezosa,
mira como ELLOS JUEGAN
y no TIENEN más que dos.

VI

La cucaracha, EN BICICLETA,
ya no puede MÁS ANDAR.
porque no tiene, porque le faltan
las dos patitas de atrás.
Cucaracha, cucaracha,
no seas tan perezosa,
mira COMO EN BICICLETA
ANDAMOS NOSOTROS DOS

The cockroach/cannot walk anymore/because it doesn't have,/because it lacks/ the two rear little legs. Cockroach, Cockroach, / don't be so lazy / look how I am walking / And I have only two.

Unit 9: En la calle

(On the street)

Suggested Materials: Toys for vehicles such as a car, a truck, a motorcycle and a bus.

1. Los vehículos

Page 38

Presenting vocabulary

- Whenever possible, introduce vocabulary with real toys. Although not in the picture, you may use words like *avión* and *tren.*

- Point to the picture and show the objects again in order to complete the vocabulary. Have children repeat the words. Then ask them, one by one: *¿Qué es esto?*
Then, proceed to more elaborate questions: *¿Cuántas personas hay en el coche? ¿De qué color es el camión? ¿Y el autobús? ¿Dónde está el perro? ¿Dónde está el gato? ¿Te gusta el coche? ¿Es bonito? ¿Te gusta la moto? ¿Qué dice el papá? ¿Que dice el chico? ¿El conductor del coche? ¿El perro?*

- Ask a child to go to the front, take a toy from your table, and ask the class: *¿Qué es?*

Page 39

Copia las palabras.

Audio-visual activity

Say the vocabulary words (or play the CD) and ask children to circle the corresponding numbers. This activity is for nouns only. Check the answers afterwards.

Hot potato

Sitting in a circle, play the game as suggested in the Appendix I.

¿Qué quieres?

- Ask children to prepare their flash cards from the Activity Book.
Alternatively, distribute magazines and ask the children to cut these objects out and glue them onto blank cards.
- Ask each child to give you some flash cards, such as *coche, camión, moto,* etc. When you have enough in your hand, you can play Vendor and Clients, asking one child at a time, *¿Qué quieres?* If the child says one of the vocabulary words, you hand him/her a flash card saying *Toma*....Remind children to use the *un* or *una* articles.

The child who collects the most flash cards becomes the vendor, and repeats the activity with the rest of the class.

Working in pairs
Same exercise as above.

Drawing
Hand out large sheets of paper and instruct children to draw a street. Then say the words for vehicles one by one for them to make their drawings, using their flashcards or magazine selections as models if needed. Be sure that they know feminine articles for *la calle* and *la motocicleta.*

2. ¡Cuidado! ¡Es peligroso!

Page 40

Presenting vocabulary.
In English, discuss with the children some situations that are *peligrosas.* Ask them what sorts of situations are "peligrosas" in their opinion. Then introduce *¡Cuidado!* and ask examples of when one must *tener cuidado.* Finally say *prohibido pasar* and ask again for examples as to where one may find these things in real life.

Writing
Ask children to copy the words beside each picture in the space provided.

¿Qué decimos?
Ask children what they would say in Spanish in certain situations. For example: a road is blocked, a person is close to a cliff, a child is handling some harmful product, etc. You want to elicit the words *es peligroso,* or *peligro, prohibido pasar,* and *cuidado.*

3. ¿Qué está haciendo?

- Teach the *–ando – iendo* endings using known verbs and actions like *escribir, dibujar, caminar, llorar.* Mimic the actions and say *¿Qué estoy haciendo? Estoy escribiendo, estoy dibujando, estoy caminando, etc.*
Do this exercise with as many different verbs as you can until the children know how to say *–ando* and *–iendo.*

- Show the two pictures and ask children to repeat the sentences written on their texts.

- Then use your puppets to represent an action. For example, dormir, caminar, llorar, and ask, *¿Qué está haciendo*? You need to elicit the *–ando* / *–iendo* endings to show action in progress.

Working in pairs
Have children mime different actions according to the vocabulary and ask his/her partner: *¿Qué estoy haciendo?*

Charade
Ask a child go to the front and, miming an action verb, ask the class: *¿Qué estoy haciendo?*

¡Yo la tengo!
Have a sheet of poster paper on the board with a picture of an empty patio or park, or draw your own patio space on the board. Ask each child to select a flash card depicting an action from their Activity Books. Make sure that there is a variety of actions. Ask children to come to the board when you say the name of the action. For example: *"Está caminando" ¿Quién tiene la figura?* The child with that action has to answer *¡Yo la tengo!* and run to affix the picture / flash card, with tape or thumbtack, as appropriate, on the board.

Page 41

Audio-visual activity
-Have children draw a circle around the numbers according to what they hear from you (or the CD):
está comiendo, está andando en bicicleta, está llorando, está durmiendo, está bebiendo, está jugando a la pelota, está caminando, está corriendo, está cruzando la calle, está diciendo "¡quiero mi chupete!", está lloviendo, está patinando.

- Then adapt the statements and questions to the pictures, and ask children to answer and converse:
1. ¿Quién está cruzando la calle? 2.¿Quién está corriendo? 3. ¿Quién está patinando? 4. ¿Quién está durmiendo? 5. ¿Quién está jugando a la pelota? 6. ¿Quién está andando en bicicleta? 7.¿ Quién está caminando? 8. Quién está comiendo? 9. ¿ Quién está tomando agua? 10. ¿Quién está llorando? 11. ¿Quién esta diciendo "dame mi chupete?" 12. ¿Y aquí ¿qué pasa?

-A variation would be to ask children the question, this time including choices. For example: *¿Qué está haciendo?¿Está caminando o comiendo?* etc.

Review:

¡Es verdad, no es verdad!
Have children collect all the flashcards of objects they have been using so far. Divide the class into groups of 3 or 4. Children take turns playing. Each child places a card on the table face down, while saying what it is. Anybody from the group can challenge, saying *"no es verdad"*. When looking at the card, if the object does not match what the child says, the one who challenged him/her can collect the card.

Other games

You can use one of the games like **Red Light Green Light, El Gran Bonetón, Jeopardy, Gallina ciega** or **Bingo** with new vocabulary.

Little rhythm

Explain the meaning of the words *tranvía* and *sandía*. Ask the students to point to themselves for the *me gusta* verses, and point to a classmate for the verses with *te gusta*, giving the interrogatory intonation. Teach the words and then listen the CD.

Me gusta ir...

Me gusta ir en moto,
¡Qué alboroto!
I like to ride a motorcycle
What a noise!
Me gusta ir en tren
¡Tracataten!
I like to go in a train
¡Tracataten!
Me gusta ir en coche
Por la noche.
I like to go by car
At night
Y en bus de mañana
(comiendo banana)
And by bus in the morning
(Eating banana)
Y andar en tranvía
Comiendo sandía.
And go in a tram
eating watermelon
¿Y andar en camión?
¡Me gusta un montón!
And to go in a truck?
I like it a lot!

¿Te gusta ir en moto
y hacer alboroto?
Do you like to ride a
motorcycle
and make lots of noise?
¿Te gusta ir en tren,
tracataten?
Do you like to go in a train,
Tracataten?
¿Te gusta ir en coche
por la noche?
Do you like to go by car
At night?
¿Y en bus de mañana.
(Comiendo banana)?
And by bus in the morning
(Eating banana)?
¿Y andar en tranvía
Comiendo sandía?
And go in a tram
eating watermelon?
¿Y andar en camión?
¡Te gusta un montón!
And to go in a truck?
You like it a lot!

Ask children to draw the vehicles in the order they appear in the stanzas. These pictures may be saved to serve as mnemonic devices.

Unit 10: Días de la semana

(Days of the week)

Suggested Materials: Construction papers, calendars

1. ¿Qué día es hoy?

- Introduce the days of the week, showing a calendar. Ask children to memorize the days. Introduce the questions: *¿Qué día es hoy? Hoy es...* *¿Qué día es mañana? Mañana es ...* Repeat the exercise every day at the beginning of class.

- Play **Hot Potato** with the days of the week.

Page 42

One by one, say the words *música, dentista, fútbol, doctor, español, parque, zoológico,* and ask children to repeat the words. Ask them to identify the pictures on p. 42 while slowly repeating the corresponding words.

Page 43

Writing

Ask children to copy the words for the days of the week in the space provided.

Matching

Then, following Luisito's schedule on p. 42, ask them to trace a line connecting the day to the pictures. For example, *jueves* will be connected to the guitar.

2. ¿Adónde va? ¿Cuándo va?

- Go to the schedule drawing in the text and ask:
¿Adónde va Luisito el lunes? Va a la escuela y al dentista.
¿Adónde va el martes? Va a la escuela y a jugar al fútbol.

- Then change your questions, using "*Cuándo*".
¿Cuándo va Luisito al dentista?

Working in pairs

Using the information from pp. 42-3, encourage children to ask these questions of each other.

Ve, vayan, ven, vengan

- Have children form a row of seven, each child representing a day of the week, from *lunes* to *domingo.* Give each child a sheet of construction paper with the name of his/her day written on it. Young children memorize their day. Draw seven squares on the board representing the days of the week, just above head level of the tallest children, so all of them can see. Then position yourself far from the board, among the students, and ask the "days" to run to the corresponding square on the board. Start with *lunes,* following the sequence, using *ve* and *vayan.* For example: *lunes, ¡ ve! Martes y miércoles, ¡vayan!*
Jueves y viernes, ¡vayan! Sabado, ¡ve! Domingo, ¡ve!
Each child has to position himself/herself under the right square.

- Repeat the exercises, but this time position yourself closer to the board and far from the students, using *ven* and *vengan.* The idea is to differentiate between *ve/vayan* vs. *ve/vengan.*

3 ¿Te gusta ir a......?

Ask children *Si* or *No* questions using "*¿Te gusta ir a...? ¿Les gustan ir a...?*
First ask the whole class *¿Les gusta ir a...?* and then ask individual students, *¿Te gusta ir a....?* to emphasize the difference between "TE" and "LES". For example:
¿Les gusta ir a la escuela? ¿a patinar? ¿al hospital?
¿ a la tienda? ¿al parque? ¿ al zoológico? ¿al restaurante? ¿al médico? ¿al dentista? ¿a la clase de español?

Page 44

Ask children to circle the number according to what they hear. (*¿Te gusta ir a......?*) Repeat the questions above in a different order (or play the CD).
Then check the answers. After the children have identified the actions, ask them to write "Si" or "No" under each picture.

¡A mí!

Have children gather flash cards from this chapter. Then ask:
¿A quién le gusta ir al zoológico? The child with the picture answers:
¡A mí me gusta! Do the same with the other actions. Also teach children to say, *¡A mí no me gusta!*

Working in pairs

Use the same pictures. One child places the pictures he/she has face down on the table. A classmate chooses one of these. The other child looks at the drawing and reacts by saying, *me gusta ir a...,* or *no me gusta ir a....*For example: *No me gusta ir al médico,* or *Me gusta ir al zoológico,* etc.

Page 45
Ask children to write, in the space provided, the days in which they have Spanish classes.

4 . Más números

Teach numbers from 10 to 40 while children look at the written numbers in their texts.
Once these are memorized, ask children to say the numbers, looking at the text if necessary.

Hot Potato
Sitting in a circle, children say the numbers in sequence, one for each student, from 1 to 40, passing the "potato".

Writing
Ask children to complete the sequence after 24 and 25 ion their texts, and then to complete the sequence after 30 saying the numbers aloud as they write them.

Audio-visual activity
Say the numbers written in the text inside the squares, in a different order, or play the CD, and ask children to circle what they hear.

Rhyme
Teach the following verse, listen to the CD and ask children to perform it in dialogue form.

- Diez, once, doce, y trece, - *Quiero comer una torta de nueces.*	*10, 11, 12, 13* *I want to eat a nut cake.*
- Catorce, quince, dieciséis, diecisiete, - *¿Tienes hambre? toma un chupete.*	*14, 15, 16, 17,* *Are you hungry? Take the pacifier.*
- Dieciocho, diecinueve, veinte y veintiuno, - *¿Dónde está? ¡ no tienes ninguno!*	*18, 19, 20, 21,* *Where is it? You don't have any!*

Voy, vas, va, vamos , van
Ask students to repeat the conjugation of *ir* to a rhythm, as on the CD: *voy, vas, va, vamos, van,* several times.

TPR
- Once students have learned the rhythmic exercises, combine the exercises with arm movements. The child says *Voy,* while touching his/her chest with both hands; *vas,* while stretching both arms forward to at another child; *va* while stretching their right arms to the right (have the children spread out so they don't touch each other); *vamos,* while making an

imaginary circle with one hand inclusive of themselves and the group; and *van* while indicating the group exclusive of themselves.
- Then say the verb in any conjugation while children perform the corresponding motions.
- Finally, do the motions while children say the verbs.

This is a good moment to introduce *nosotros* and *ellas/ellos (ustedes* will be taught later).

Al ritmo de "Voy – vas - va - vamos - van"
Play the CD until children learn it. (It may take several days.)
Before each verse, children say the personal pronoun aloud, as on the CD.

YO
Voy siempre a la escuela,
si llueve y si hace sol
Y canto todo el día
en inglés y en español. (1)

TÚ
Vas siempre a la escuela,
si llueve y si hace sol,
Y cantas todo el día
en inglés y en español.

ÉL *or* ELLA
Va ella a la escuela
si llueve y si hace sol,
Y canta todo el día
en inglés y en español.

NOSOTROS
Vamos a la escuela
si llueve y si hace sol,
Cantamos todo el día
en inglés y en español.

ELLOS
Van siempre a la escuela
si llueve y si hace sol,
Y cantan todo el día
en inglés y en español.

[1] I always go to school / if it rains or if it is sunny/ I sing all day long / in English and in Spanish.

Have children accompany each verse with hand movements, signaling the five personal pronouns

Bingo
Provide students with old calendars. Ask them to cut out any numbers from 1 to 31 and glue them at random on a bingo sheet (so that each student has 16 of the 31 numbers).

Play any other game like **Gallina ciega, Jeopardy** or **Red light Green light.**

Unit 11: El calendario

(The calendar)

Suggested Materials: Construction paper. A current calendar

1. ¿Cuándo es tu cumpleaños?

Page 46

Presenting vocabulary

Teach children the 12 months, looking at the 12 calendars illustrated in their texts.

Finding their birthdays

Children already know the word *cumpleaños* from Unit 4. Ask each child to find, on p.46, the calendar that corresponds to the month of his/her birthday. Tell them that each month corresponds to a number (for example, *agosto* will be #8) so that it will be easy for children who do not yet read to find their month. Afterwards, ask children to put the first letters of each of the days of the week in sequential order in the month that corresponds to their birthdays. (Write on the board the D for *domingo,* L for *lunes,* M for *martes,* M for *miércoles,* etc.)
Ex: if a *cumpleaños* is in February, the second calendar will be marked with the letters:

L	M	M	J	V	S	D

Then, using a current calendar, you can help them determine which day of the week is their birthday and write the number in the space for that day. Try to do this activity using as much Spanish as you can.
At the end of this exercise, each student will have his/her own birthday written in the corresponding month. For example:

L	M	M	J	V	S	D
			1			

Page 47

Based on the previous exercise, teach children how to say a date. For example: *4 de julio*. Then ask each of them to say the date of their birthday.

Writing
Ask children to fill in the blanks with their answers to the questions:
_ *¿Cuándo es tu cumpleaños? ¿Cuántos años cumples?*

Mi cumpleaños es el ... de ....   *Cumplo ....años*

Proceed with the other dates given on their text.
You may add holiday dates as appropriate, according to your group's composition.

2. ¿Qué fecha es hoy?

Ask the children to write on the calendar (p.46) the number corresponding to *"la fecha de hoy"*. Ascertaining where the number belongs will constitute practice in learning the days of the week. You can help the children by pointing to the current calendar.

Hot potato
Sitting in a circle, play hot potato using birthdays. Each children has to say *"Mi cumpleaños es el... de.............."*

3. Las estaciones

Teach the four seasons using the pictures in the text and others from calendars or magazines.

Drawing
Ask children to draw their own *árbol en primavera (con flores), árbol en verano (con hojas verdes), árbol en otoño (con hojas amarillas y marrones) y un árbol en invierno (sin hojas),* or have children find corresponding pictures in magazines.

Page 48

4. La temperatura

- Show the temperature on each thermometer in the illustration to teach *hace frío* and *hace calor.* (Point out the difference between "calor" for weather and *"caliente"* for food, liquids or objects.)
- Then, teach *tengo frío* and *tengo calor* with arm motions (cuddling or fanning yourself). Ask children to imitate you.
- Go back to the seasonal pictures on p. 47 and say:

Es verano ¿Hace frío o hace calor?   *Es Invierno ¿Hace frío o hace calor?*

Más números

- Introduce the numbers as you did the previous ones, by repetition, paying attention to the difference between 60 and 70.

-Ask questions about peoples' ages. For example:

Laura (on p. 18) *¿tiene 6 años o tiene 60 años?*
Y Luisito ¿tiene 7 años o 70 años?
Y tú ¿tienes 5 años o 50?
Y yo ¿tengo 4 años o 40 años?
Y tu mamá (or papá) ¿ cuántos años tiene?
Y el abuelo, ¿ tiene 8 años u 80 años?

- Draw a large thermometer on the board with degrees in increments of 10 from 30 to 100. Point to different numbers and ask?

¿Cuántos grados hace? ¿Hace frío o hace calor?

- Summarize the use of the two verbs, saying:

Cuando hace frío, yo tengo frío. Cuando hace calor, yo tengo calor.
¿ En Alaska hace frío? Sí, hace frío.
¿Y el oso tiene frío? No, no tiene frío. ¡Al oso le gusta el frío!
¿En verano hace calor? Sí, hace calor.
¿Y el mosquito tiene calor? No, no tiene calor. ¡Al mosquito le gusta el calor!
¿Y ustedes tienen frío? ¿Les gusta el frío o el calor?

Writing

Looking at the numbers, children decide which one is *"frío"* or *"calor"*. Ask them to complete the sentences copying the words from the board.

Dialogue

Teach the following traditional children's sayings:

- *Tengo frío*	-*Ponte el sombrero de tu tío*
- *Tengo calor*	- *Ponte el ventilador*

After students have memorized these traditional dialogic rhymes, ask them to think about possible answers to the statements *tengo frío* and *tengo calor*

-Examples for *tengo frío: ponte el suéter, ponte la chaqueta, ponte el sombrero, ponte las medias.*
-Examples for *tengo calor: toma un helado, toma un jugo.*

More expressions with "tengo..."

-Ask children to mimic, as everyone repeats: *tengo frío,* (hugging themselves, shivering), *tengo calor,* (fanning themselves), *tengo hambre* (touching their tummies), *tengo sed* (pointing to their mouths or throats). This will be a good occasion to introduce *tengo sueño.* Closing your eyes, pillow your head on your hands and ask children to do the same.

-Then reverse the exercise, mimicking one of the above sensations and asking children *¿Qué tengo?*

Review activities

Page 49

Audio-visual exercise.
Ask children to circle the number above each of the four drawings according to the season and the temperature they hear. For example, you (or the CD) will say: *es el verano, es el invierno, hace frío, hace calor, es primavera, es el otoño, es el 25 de diciembre, es el 4 de julio*...(some numbers will have several circles).

¿Qué número es?
Ask children to circle the number they hear.

Associations
Ask children to cut out the flash cards depicting seasons from the Activity Book and place them on their table together with pictures they have cut out of magazines and their own drawings. Then say different sentences associated with the weather, and have them show the class some pictures they can associate with your statement.

Poem
Teach the poem below. Ask children to look at the two pictures on p. 49 and to fill in the space after *Hace* for each illustration. Then ask the class *¿Quién habla en el poema?* (The answer is, of course, the dog!)

¡Qué bueno el verano!

¡Qué bueno el verano	*How good is the Summer*
Porque hay mucho sol!	*because there is lots of sun!*
Me meto en el agua	*I get into the water*
Si tengo calor.	*If I feel warm*
¡Qué bueno el verano,	*How good is the Summer*
porque hay mucho sol!	*because there is lots of sun!*
¡Qué bueno el invierno!	*How good is the Winter!*
Me río y me río.	*I laugh and laugh.*
Me meto en la cama	*I get into bed*
Si yo tengo frío	*If I feel cold.*
¡Qué bueno el invierno!	*How good is the Winter!*
Me río y me río	*I laugh and laugh*
Otoño y primavera,	*Fall and Spring*
me gustan las dos.	*I like both.*
Yo no tengo frío	*I am not cold*
Ni tengo calor.	*Nor I am hot.*
Yo tengo a mi amigo	*I have my friend*
en mi corazón.	*In my heart.*

Unit 12: ¡Al aire libre!

(Outdoors!)

1. Vamos al zoológico

<u>Suggested materials</u>: animal toys (elephant, giraffe, camel, deer, horse, snake, lion, crocodile, tiger, turtle, rabbit, monkey, fish, worm, bee, butterfly, fly and any domestic animal). Gold and silver paper (wrapping paper, for instance) and large blue and black art paper.

Page 50

Presenting vocabulary

Use your toys as well as the illustration on p.50 to teach the names of animals.
Most of these animal words are cognates, so children will have little difficulty in learning them fast. Once they recognize them, say:

Miren el dibujo. El león y el tigre son animales carnívoros. ¿Qué dicen el tigre y el león? Dicen ¡Vamos a comer a los animales!
Pero los otros animales, on the other side of the fence, *se ríen:¡ ja ja ja, ji ji ji..!*
¿Por qué se ríen? Porque...el león y el tigre no pueden pasar por las rejas (cannot go through the fence).
Then ask the questions:
¿Cómo se ríe el elefante? ¿Cómo se ríe el camello? ¿Cómo se ríe el caballo?
¿Cómo te ríes tú? ¿Como (like) *el elefante o como el caballo?*

Page 51

Audio-visual activity

Ask children to circle the number corresponding to the animal you (or the CD) say.

¿Qué animal es?

Ask students to cut out several flash cards depicting animals they have just learned, and place them on the table. Then say a few sentences. Children identify the animal you have mentioned. For example:
- *¡Animal carnívoro!* Children should look for a carnivorous animal and show the card to the class, saying, for example, *el león.*
- *¡Come zanahorias* (carrots)! Children show, and say, *el conejo* or *el caballo.*
- *¡Come insectos!* Children show, and say, *la araña.*

2. El día y la noche

Presenting vocabulary

- Draw a sun, a moon, some stars and some clouds on the board to teach these words, and ask children to repeat them.

- Divide the board in three parts. In one show a sun on the horizon, and say:
Es de mañana. Sale el sol.
In the second draw a sun high in the sky and say: *Es de tarde.*
In the third draw a half moon and say: *Es de noche.*

- Then tell children different times, for example, it is 8:00 AM, it is 2:00 PM, it is 11:00 PM, and ask them:
¿Es de mañana, de tarde o de noche?

Artwork: *El día y la noche*
Give the children two large sheets of paper, one blue and one black, and some gold and silver paper, and ask them to make *el día* and *la noche.* For example, *el día* might be done on blue construction paper with a gold paper sun and white paper clouds. Help children draw the clouds, if necessary, so they can cut them out. *La noche* can be done on black paper and may have stars and the moon made of silver paper. Children may complete this artwork later on after they know more nature vocabulary, such as that on p. 52.

3. Un picnic en el campo

Page 52

Presenting vocabulary
-Show the illustration on p.52 and ask children:
¿Es de día o de noche? ¿Cuántas personas hay en el picnic?¿Cuántos chicos hay? ¿Hay un abuelo? ¿Hay animales? ¿Hay pájaros? ¿Hay flores? ¿Hay sol? ¿Hay animales grandes? ¿Hay insectos?

- Introduce the new words, using them in sentences. For example:

- *La montaña es blanca. Tiene nieve. ¿Hay montañas aquí en .....* ? (give the name your town or city).
- *Estos son los pajaritos. La mamá pájara les da gusanos* (show the other *gusano* on the leaf).
¿Nosotros comemos gusanos? ¿Quién come gusanos?
-*El abuelo y el niño están cocinando salchichas en el fuego. ¿A ustedes les gusta comer salchichas?*
- Then show the mountain, the bird, the worm and the fire and ask *¿Cómo se dice....?*
- Proceed with new sentences:

- *La mamá, el papá y el niño están mirando el río. Aquí hay un señor en el río. Está pescando. Hay peces en el río. El niño mira el pez* (explain the difference between *pez* and *pescado*). Then ask *¿Hay un río aquí en.... ?* (give the name of the town or city where you live).
¿Quién tiene peces en su casa? ¿ Quién tiene pecera?
Then show the river, the fish, the mountain, the fire, etc., and ask *¿Cómo se dice...?*

- Point to the other figures and say:
El gusano está en la hoja. La abeja está en la flor. La mosca está en la tierra. Los pajaritos están en el nido. El nido está en el árbol.
Then show the bee, the nest and the tree, and ask *¿Dónde está el gusano? ¿Dónde está la abeja? ¿Dónde está la mosca? ¿Dónde están los pajaritos? ¿Dónde está el nido?*

- Indicate the different actions and say
La abeja está comiendo el néctar de la flor. La mariposa está volando.
La mosca, la mariposa, los pájaros y la abeja vuelan. ¿El gusano vuela? ¿El pez vuela? ¿El niño vuela?

¿Dónde viven?

Flash card activity

Review all the vocabulary and ask children to prepare their flash cards from the Activity Book. Then ask them to group animals that know how to fly, that live in the water, that eat meat, that eat plants, etc.
Children show the class their flash cards according to what they hear. For example:
Animales que vuelan. Animales que viven en el agua. Animales que viven en los árboles, etc.

Making sentences

Ask children to make their own sentences while looking at the drawings for *¿Dónde viven?* and listening to your questions:
- *¿Dónde vive el pájaro?*
- *¿Dónde vive la tortuga?*
- *¿Dónde viven las personas? ¿Dónde vives tú?*

Writing

Ask children to write the name of the animals and habitats in the spaces provided. For example:

pájaro/ nido *tortuga / agua* *casa*

Red light Green light

With the vocabulary just learned, play the Red Light/Green Light game according to the explanations in the appendix. You can use two groups of animals categorized according to their eating habits; for example, the carnivores and the vegetarians will make two different categories. You can use *animales que vuelan, animales peligrosos,* etc.

Page 53

Audio-visual activity

Ask children to circle the numbers according to what they hear and then check the answers.

árboles – abeja – gusano – flores – hoja – fuego – río – nido – montaña

Audio-visual and speaking activity: a escuchar y decir. ¿Qué animal es?

Ask children to name the animal you are describing. Use animals represented in the 12 illustrations. You may use sentences such as:

1- *Este animal vive en el agua y en la tierra. Cuando camina, lleva su casa.* (turtle)
2- *Este animal vuela, vive en los árboles y come gusanos y semillas.* (seeds) (bird)
3- *Este insecto vuela, tiene 6 patas y es color anaranjado y negro.* (bee)
4- *Este animal es el más grande de todos los animales.* (elephant)
5- *Este animal vive en el agua solamente.* (fish)
6- *Este animal tiene muchas patas, y come insectos. A veces es peligroso para las personas.* (spider)
7- *Este animal vive en la tierra y en los árboles. No tiene patas. A veces es peligroso.*(snake)
8- *Este animal vive en la tierra y en el agua. Tiene muchos dientes peligrosos.* (crocodile)
9- *Este insecto vuela, es molesto, le gusta comer cosas dulces y cosas que no están buenas.* (fly)
10- *Este animal corre rápido, tiene orejas grandes y le gustan los vegetales.* (rabbit)
11- *Este animal vive en la tierra. No tiene patas.* (worm)
12- *Este animal vive en la jungla. Come carne.* (tiger)

Bingo!

Ask children to cut and color the small animal pictures and glue them on a bingo sheet. There are more than 12 animals in this lesson, so not all of them will have to be on all the bingo sheets, but make sure that all of them are represented in the class, and that the children glue them randomly.

Hot potato

Sitting in a circle, play the game as suggested in the Appendix. You could add other animals if you have them among your toys, such as *gallina, pato* and *cerdo* (or *chancho).*

Song

Teach the song (next page) and listen to it in the CD.

To help with memorization, let children listen to one stanza at a time and ask them to draw each animal as it is mentioned. Then have them listen to the songs while looking at their own drawings, until they memorize the words.

Start by teaching the words that are not part of previous vocabulary.

Corre que corre

I		II	
Corre que corre La linda jirafa Dos piernas cortas Y dos piernas largas. Corre que corre La linda jirafa No tiene miedo de correr.	*It runs and runs, the pretty giraffe Two short legs and two long legs It runs and runs, the pretty giraffe, she is not afraid of running.*	Camina lento La tortuguita Porque ella tiene La pata cortita. Camina lento La tortuguita Pero camina sin parar.	*It walks and does not run, The little turtle Because she has short little legs It walks and does not run, The little turtle, but she walks without stopping.*
III		**IV**	
Trota que trota El elefante Con una trompa Muy elegante. Trota que trota El elefante Con sus orejas de gran señor	*It trots and trots, the elephant With a trumpet very elegant (He) trots and trots, the elephant with his ears of grand Lord*	Duerme que duerme La bella serpiente No tiene patas ¡Pero tiene dientes! Duerme que duerme La bella serpiente Si hace frío o calor.	*It sleeps and sleeps, the beautiful snake, It doesn't have legs but it has teeth! It sleeps and sleeps, the beautiful snake, if it is cold and if it is hot.*
V		**VI**	
Vuela que vuela La mariposa Vuela en el campo De rosa en rosa. Vuela que vuela La mariposa Vuela en el campo de flor en flor.	*It flies and flies, the butterfly Flies in the fields from rose to rose It flies and flies, the butterfly Flies in the fields from flower to flower*	Llora que llora El cocodrilo, Y tiene dientes Con mucho filo. Llora y muerde El cocodrilo, ¡Nunca te bañes cerca de él!	*It cries and cries. The crocodile And he has very sharp teeth It cries and bite the crocodile, Never bathe near him!*
VII		**VIII**	
Anda el mono En la bicicleta Y anda el gorila En la motoneta. Anda el mono En la bicicleta Y anda la mona en monopatín	*(He) rides, the monkey, on the bicycle. And (he) rides, the gorilla, in the motorcycle. (He) rides, the monkey, on the bicycle and (she)rides, the she monkey on a skateboard.*	Pone un huevo La gallinita Para las Pascuas De mañanita. Pone un huevo La gallinita Para las Pascuas y para ti.	*Lays an egg the little hen, for Easter early in the morning. Lays an egg the little hen, for Easter and for you.*
IX		**X**	
Mira que lindo Se puso el día, Y aquí termina Nuestra poesía.	*Look how beautiful the day turned out, And here we finish our poesy.*	Mira que lindo Se puso el día. ¡Vamos afuera por fin a jugar!	*Look how beautiful the day turned out, Let's go outside to play at last!*

Audio-visual and writing activity
Ask children to circle the number according to what they hear, and then to write the words accordingly. For the first row of illustrations (1-3), say the words
sol, estrella, luna.
For the second row (4-6), say:
Es de noche. En el cielo está la luna y hay muchas estrellas.
Es de tarde. Hay nubes y sol en el cielo.
Es de mañana. Hay nubes en el cielo pero no hay sol.

Ask children to copy *mañana, tarde, noche,* after you say these words.

Finish the artwork: el día y la noche

Play ***Es verdad, no es verdad,*** as explained in Appendix I.

4. ¿Qué decimos?

Introduce *Buenos días, Buenas tardes* and *Buenas noches* pointing at the illustrations.

Then say:
Es de mañana. Hay un pajarito en la ventana. El sol está saliendo. ¿Qué decimos?
Es de tarde. El sol está alto en el cielo. ¿Qué decimos?
Es de noche. Hay estrellas en el cielo. ¿Qué decimos?

Ahora, es el fin de la clase. ¿Qué decimos?

¡Adiós amiguitos!

You can finish the school year by presenting a play. See our adaptation of **Little Red Riding Hood (*Caperucita Roja*)** in Appendix I (p. 59) which will be easily followed by parents.

Appendix I

Games and activities for all occasions

This and the following games can be played at any time. Each reinforces vocabulary given prior to the game and stimulates concentration and enthusiasm at any stage of learning.

Red Light Green Light

A student, or the instructor, stands in front of the class facing a row of children standing side by side in a row separated by as many steps as practical from the leader.
The leader announces the identities of the red light and the green light. A simple form of the game is to use, for example, animal names as one light and names of things -- fruit, for instance, as the other.
The leader then says a word. If the word is a fruit the children advance. They stop when the leader says the name of an animal.
Of course, the identities of the red and green lights should change as the children learn new vocabulary

Hide and Seek

Before class, hide a variety of figurines and toys from your Magic Box around the classroom. When the children come in, have them search for the toys. Give hints to children who are not finding any. Once all or most things have been discovered, bring the students into a circle and have them count in Spanish objects they have found. Go through all the names of the objects, asking students to repeat the names in Spanish.

Bingo

To play bingo children cut out the bingo sheets or grids from their Activity Books. Then they select the small pictures according to the theme, cut them out and glue them randomly on the sheet. Make sure the pictures are placed at random so everyone will have a different board. Provide beans to put on the squares. One child will announce the words from a list of words (looking at the pictures provided by the teacher). The first student who finishes the first row can be the next announcer.

Jeopardy

Divide the class into two teams and make sure there are kids of all levels on each team (don't let them choose their own teams). Have them choose Spanish team names, such as "Los Burros!" Ask Spanish questions of each team. For example, for Unit 4 (about family and parties), ask questions such as: "What does ***regalos*** mean?" Make the questions increasingly difficult, such as "What does ***Laura tiene 6 años*** mean?" Mark each team point on the board as questions are answered correctly.

A Variation of Jeopardy. Questions can be from English to Spanish. For example, the teacher may ask ***¿Cómo se dice…book?*** Single words or expressions such as ***ball, bike, take, give me, thank you,*** etc., may be used.

Spanish Basquetbol

This game is the same as jeopardy, except that each time a team member answers correctly, they get to take a "shot" and, if they make it, the team gets a point. (Set up a basket and a stuffed animal or ball to throw.)

Spanish tag

(Works best outside.) Choose the vocabulary of the lesson being studied. You can choose food, for example, as your category. Everyone runs away from the person who is "it" and if a student ducks down on the floor and says a food-related word in Spanish, such as ***plato, sal, leche,*** etc., they cannot be tagged. They can only stay down for 2 seconds, however, and then have to get up and run again. Each child can only say each word once (i.e., cannot repeat the same word every time).

La gallina ciega (The blind chicken)

To play *La gallina ciega* you need to use objects from your "Caja mágica" (teaching materials box).

Collect 8 or 10 objects (one for each child in the group). Divide the class into small groups. Children form a circle, each child holding an object except for the child who is acting as the *gallina ciega*. This child is blindfolded. The teacher turns the *gallina ciega* child around a few times and then asks him/her to walk toward a classmate in the circle. The chosen child in the circle will hand his/her object to the *gallina ciega* and ask ***¿Qué es?*** The *gallina ciega* has to guess what the object is in Spanish, or say ***"ayuda"*** if he/she doesn't know.

The other children can, with the teacher's help, provide clues. For example, they may say: *es un animal, es un vehículo, es ropa, es una comida, es una fruta.* They may add colors or any other clue that is part of their vocabulary.

The child whose object was chosen will be the next *gallina ciega*.

Hot potato with objects

To play *Papa Caliente* with the vocabulary you have just covered, start by throwing one object to a student in the circle, and say the name in Spanish. The student who has the new toy then throws one of the old toys to a different classmate in the circle and says the name in Spanish.

The 2nd student keeps the new toy and throws an old toy to a 3rd classmate in the circle while saying its name in Spanish. Continue doing this until everyone has a new batch of toys. If a student forgets an object's name, see if one of the other students can help out.

Hot potato can be played with abstract nouns, such as numbers, colors, or full sentences, such as *"Mi cumpleaños es..."*

El Gran Bonetón

Ask children to gather all of the flash cards they have been using so far.
Each child is given a conical hat, all of different colors. The teacher plays first with a card that nobody has. After all the children have played, the teacher takes another card. Each student has to look at their cards to see if they have what the teacher (*El Gran Bonetón*) is saying.
The teacher starts the speech:

Gran Bonetón: *El Gran Bonetón perdió* (lost) *su ....bicicleta. Y dice que el bonete blanco* (for example) *la tiene.*

Bonete Blanco: *¿Yo señor?*

Gran Bonetón: *¡Sí señor!*

Bonete Blanco: *¡No señor!*

Gran Bonetón: *Y entonces, ¿Quién la tiene?*

Bonete Blanco: *El bonete...¡amarillo!* (for example - they can choose any *bonete*).

Bonete amarillo: *¿Yo señor?*

Bonete Blanco: *¡ Sí señor!*

Bonete amarillo: *¡No señor!*

Bonete Blanco: *Y entonces, ¿Quién la tiene?*

Bonete amarillo: *El bonete ...* and he/she will choose another classmate with a different *bonete.* On the second round, if the *bonete* has the object, he/she will say: *¡Yo la tengo!* and will be the next *Gran Bonetón.*

¡Es verdad, no es verdad!

This game works well at the end of the year after children have collected many flash cards from the activity books so that they have more than one of the same.
Divide the class into groups of 3 or 4. Groups play independently.
One player starts the game by putting a card face down while saying the name of the object it represents. The player may or may not be bluffing. Let's say that the child says *silla*. Everybody else has to continue putting a card face down and saying *silla*. They may or may not have a *silla* in reality. The pile of cards in the center will keep growing until at any point in the game someone in the group challenges by saying: *no lo creo* (I don't believe you). At this point, the card in question has to be displayed. If the object is not a *silla,* then the one that bluffed has to collect all the cards from the pile. If the player was telling the truth and the object is a *silla,* the challenger collects the cards. The player who ends up with no cards is the winner.

Storytelling

Choose a good Spanish or bilingual story (such as the bilingual Hoopoe books suggested in our website) and read one sentence at a time, first in English, then in Spanish. Periodically stop and ask, for example, *¿Qué quiere decir "perro"?* or whatever characters, animals, or objects you have just read in English. This is a very good way for children to learn new words.

Spanish movie

Show the Spanish version of an English language movie, preferably one that they have seen (like *The Little Mermaid*). Periodically pause the Spanish version and vocalize a simple phrase or word that has just been said by a character in the movie. Rewind a bit and play the scene again so that the children can practice their recognition of the phrase or word. Have a sheet of paper numbered from 1-50 beforehand for the children to write down words as the film goes on. Set a goal, such as learning 50 different words.

Drama time

Children perform a short play, either using puppets if you have them, or acting the parts themselves. You may have children dressed as the characters in the story.
The following is an example of a traditional story adapted for use in children's Spanish classes.

***Caperucita Roja* (Little Red Riding Hood)**
This play is appropriate for practicing parts of the body, names of fruits, and the verb "ir."
Props: for the wolf: mustaches, a tail, big ears and nose made with cardboard; for grandmother: a scarf and glasses; a red scarf for Little Red Riding hood. Also: plastic fruits, cookies and a basket.

PRIMER ACTO: EN EL BOSQUE
Caperucita enters, singing *la laa la laa, la laa la laa....*
El lobo intercepts her.
Lobo: *¿Adónde vas, Caperucita?*
Caperucita: *Voy a la casa de mi abuelita.*
Lobo: *¿Y dónde vive tu abuelita?*
Caperucita: *Allá en la casita...(*pointing to a faraway place at the end of the classroom).
Lobo: *¿Y qué tienes en la cesta?*
Caperucita: (as she gathers plastic fruit and cookies) *Mira, tengo manzanas, bananas, naranjas,...Son para mi abuelita que está enferma.*
Lobo: *Bueno,¡ Adiós!*
The *lobo* leaves the scene, running and rubbing his hands together.

SEGUNDO ACTO: EN LA CASA
Place some chairs together as scenery to make the *casa de la abuelita.*
Lobo: (knocking at a fictitious door) *Knock knock.*
Abuela: (from the other side of the chairs) *¿Quién es?*
Lobo: (simulating a child's voice) *Soy yo abuela, Caperucita.*
Abuela: (looking through the window) *¡No, no! ¡Tú eres el lobo malo!*

Grandmother hides under a table. The *lobo* finds a scarf, puts it on his head and lays down on the floor covering himself with a blanket.

TERCER ACTO: EN LA CASA
Caperucita: (at the door of grandma's house) *¡Knock Knock!*
Lobo: (simulating grandma's voice) *¿Quién es?*
Caperucita: *¡Soy yo, abuelita, Caperucita. Tengo frutas y galletas para ti.*
Lobo: *Entra, Caperucita.*
Caperucita: *Hola abuela. ¿Cómo estás? Pero...¡qué ojos grandes tienes!*
Lobo: *Para mirarte mejor, Caperucita.*
Caperucita: *Pero...abuelita... ¡qué orejas grandes tienes!*
Lobo: *Para escucharte mejor, Caperucita.*

Caperucita: *Pero…abuelita, ¡qué boca grande tienes!*
Lobo: *Para hablarte mejor, Caperucita.*
Caperucita: *Pero…abuelita, ¡qué dientes grande tienes!*
Lobo: *Para….*
Abuela:(at this point grandma comes out of her hiding place and screams): *¡ Lobo malo! ¡Lobo tonto! ¡Lobo ridículo! ¡Lobo estúpido! ¡Vete, vete!* (while hitting the *lobo* with her scarf…and the *lobo* leaves the scene running , saying *Uy uy uy,* with the two women after him).

Appendix II

GLOSSARY FOR PARENTS

A

abrazo = *embrace* , hug
abuela = *grandmother*
abuelo = *grandfather*
abuelos = *grandparents*
actividad = *activity*
adiós = *goodbye*
agua = *water*
aire libre = *open air*
amarillo= *yellow*
amigo = *friend*
anaranjado = *orange*
años = *years*
araña = *spider*
árbol = *tree*
arco iris = *rainbow*
auto = *car*
autobús = *bus*
azúcar = *sugar*
azul= *blue*

B

bañera = *bathtub*
baño = *bathroom*
barriga = *belly*
bebe = *he / she drinks*
bebé = *baby*
beso = *kiss*
bicicleta = *bicycle, bike*
bien = *well*
blanco = *white*
boca = *mouth*
bonito = *pretty*
brazos = *arms*
bueno = *good*

C

caballo = *horse*
cabeza = *head*
calcetines = *socks*
calendario = *calendar*
caliente = *hot*
calle = *street*
calor = *heat* hace calor = *It is hot (weather)*
cama = *bed*
camello = *camel*
camión = *truck*

camisa = ***shirt***
camiseta = ***t-shirt***
canción = ***song***
cansado = ***tired***
cara = ***face***
caramelos = ***candy***
casa = ***house***
ciervo = ***deer***
cocina = ***kitchen***
cocodrilo = ***crocodile***
coche = ***car***
color = ***color***
comedor = ***dining room***
come = ***he / she eats***
comer = ***to eat***
conductor = ***driver***
conejo = ***rabbit***
contento = ***glad***
corre = ***he / she runs***
cuaderno = ***notebook***
cuándo = ***when***
cuarto = ***room***
cuchara = ***spoon***
cuchillo = ***knife***
cuentos = ***stories***
cuerpo = ***body***
cuidado = ***be careful***
cumpleaños = ***birthday***

Ch

chaqueta = ***jacket***
chico = ***small boy***
chupete = ***pacifier***

D

dedos = ***fingers***
día = ***day***
dice = ***he / she says***
dientes = ***teeth***
domingo = ***Sunday***
dormitorio = ***bedroom***
duerme = ***he / she sleeps***

E

edificio = ***building***
el = ***the***
él = ***he***
elefante = ***elephant***
ella = ***she***
enojado = ***mad, angry***
escalera = ***stairs***
escritorio = ***desk***
escuela = ***school***
estaciones = ***seasons***

estómago = *stomach*
estrella = *star*
extraterrestre = *extraterrestrial*

F

falda = *skirt*
familia = *family*
fecha = *date*
feo = *ugly*
fiesta = *party*
flores = *flowers*
frío = *cold*

G

gato = *cat*
globos = *balloons*
goma = *eraser*
gorro = *cap*
gracias = *thank you*
grande = *big*
gris = *grey*

H

hacer = to do
hace calor = *It is hot (weather)*
hace frío = *It is cold (weather)*
hay = *there is / there are*
helado= *ice cream*
hermana = *sister*
hermano = *brother*
hola = *hello*
hoy = *today*
huevos = *eggs*

I

invierno = *winter*

J

jabón = *soap*
jardín = *garden*
jirafa = *giraffe*
jueves = *Thursday*
jugo = *juice*

L

lago = *lake*
lápiz = *pencil*
leche = *milk*
lee = *he /she reads*
león = *lion*
libro = *book*
luna = *moon*
lunes = *Monday*
luz = *light*

LL

llueve = *it rains*

M

mal = *bad*
mamá = *mother, mom*
manos = *hands*
manzanas = *apples*
mañana = *morning / tomorrow*
mariposa = *butterfly*
marrón = *brown*
martes = *Tuesday*
mesa = *table*
meses = *months*
mi = *my*
miércoles = *Wednesday*
mono = *monkey*
mosca = *fly*
moto = *motorcycle*
muebles = *furniture*
muñeca = *doll*

N

naranja = *orange*
nariz = *nose*
negro = *black*
nena = *girl*
nene = *boy*
nido = *nest*
noche = *night*
nube = *cloud*
números = *numbers*

O

ojos = *eyes*
ombligo = *navel*
orejas = *ears*
oso = *bear*
otoño = *fall, autumn*

P

pájaro = *bird*
pan = *bread*
pantalón = *pants, trousers*
papá = *father, dad*
papas fritas = *french fries*
papel = *paper*
parque = *park*
pasar = *to spend / to pass / to happen*
pastel = *pie, cake*
patina = *he / she skates*
patines = *roller skates*
peligroso = *dangerous*
pelo = *hair*
pelota = *ball*
pequeño = *small*
perro = *dog*

pescado = *fish*
pez = *fish*
pies = *feet*
piernas = *legs*
piso = *floor*
plato = *plate*
pollo = *chicken*
primavera = *spring*
primos = *cousins*
puerta = *door*

Q

queso = *cheese*

R

ratón = *mouse*
regalo = *present, gift*
regla = *ruler*
rojo = *red*
ropa = *clothes*
rosado = *pink*
ruido = *noise*

S

sábado = *Saturday*
sala = *living room*
semáforo = *traffic lights*
señor = *mister*
señora = *Mrs., missis, madam*
serpiente = *snake, serpent*
silla = *chair*
sillón = *armchair*
sol = *sun*
sombrero = *hat*
sopa = *soup*

T

tarde = *afternoon / late*
taza = *cup*
tenedor = *fork*
tener = *to have*
tener calor = *to be hot*
tener frío = *to be cold*
tener hambre = *to be hungry*
tener sed = *to be thirsty*
tía = *aunt*
tienda = *store*
tigre = *tiger*
tío = *uncle*
toalla = *towel*
torta = *cake*
tortuga = *turtle*
triciclo = *tricycle*
triste = *sad*
tu = *your*

tú = *you*

U

uva = *grape*

V

va = *he / she goes*
vamos = *we go*
vas = *you go*
vaso = *glass*
vehículos = *vehicles*
velas = *candles*
ventana = *window*
verano = *summer*
verde = *green*
vestido = *dress*
viernes = *Friday*
violeta = *violet*
voy = *I go*

Y

yo = *I*

Z

zapatilla (tenis) = *tennis shoes*
zapatos = *shoes*